TRINIDAD HIGH SCHOOL
LIBRARY

Practical Self-Defense For Women

A Manual
Of Prevention
And Escape
Techniques

by

Judith A.H. Luchsinger

DILLON PRESS, INC.
MINNEAPOLIS, MINNESOTA

©1977 and 1978 by Dillon Press, Inc. All rights reserved

Dillon Press, Inc., 500 South Third Street
Minneapolis, Minnesota 55415

Printed in the United States of America

Library of Congress Cataloging in Publication Data

Luchsinger, Judith A. H.
   Practical self-defense for women.

   Includes bibliographical references.
   1. Self-defense for women.   I. Title.
[GV1111.5.L8   1978]   796.8'1   78-2277
ISBN 0-87518-160-0

Contents

Introduction 5

Chapter I   Mental Preparedness 7

Chapter II   What is Self-Defense? 11

Chapter III   Prevention and Preparedness 15

Chapter IV   Pressure Points & Vulnerable Areas 20

Chapter V   Escape Techniques 27

Daily Lesson Plans 39

Chapter VI   Falling Techniques 57

Chapter VII   A Throwing Technique 71

Chapter VIII   Advanced Techniques 75

Chapter IX   Conclusion 90

To Viv, whose help was invaluable throughout the book.

Acknowledgments:
Gary Knox, Photography
Polly Kielkucki, First Subject
Viv Rengstorff, Second Subject
Waterloo Courier, *Tim Cochran, Photographer* (page 6)

Introduction

This book grew out of my twelve years of experience as a teacher of self-defense methods and techniques. Time and again it has been brought to my attention that there is too little material available on practical self-defense techniques for women and girls. There are too few classes on the subject and almost no written instructions on how one can help prevent an attack, or escape from the assailant if an attack occurs. Planned programs in self-defense are valuable to women's groups as well as to public and private organizations concerned with adult education. They should be a part of every junior high or senior high curriculum, and they belong on our college campuses.

My personal awareness of the need for a practical course in self-defense came one day when, as I was walking up a stairway to a women's lounge, a man attacked me and tried to pin me against the railing. Because of my years of participation in the sport of judo, I was able to ward off the attack and throw the man down the stairs. But what of the women who have had no judo training? Most women would have been absolutely helpless in that situation. I had competed in both brown- and black-belt divisions of judo and enjoyed spending the time and energy needed to gain proficiency in the sport; but what about the millions of women who have neither the time for nor the interest in such sports? What are their alternatives?

Realizing that the answer for the majority of women would be a *practical* course in self-defense, I developed a course centered around the fact that today, with the increasing number of rapes and other assaults, self-defense is a necessity for *all* women—from the junior high level to senior citizens.

In this manual you will find the results of my experience in teaching women's self-defense classes. Some of the throws and other techniques have been borrowed from judo, aikido, and other sports, but they have been specially adapted for women's use. In this book, you will learn how to counter physical strength with speed, agility, and special techniques that utilize many different parts of the body.

Daily lesson plans for a 27-day course are included in the center of the book to help readers set up an instructional program based on the use of this manual.

All of the techniques described here require practice, but there are also valuable suggestions and preventive measures that can be put to immediate use.

To my knowledge, this is the first manual of its kind. In my years of teaching self-defense I have never found a reference that outlined a program of skills and techniques that are practical for the majority of women. For this reason, and for all those who have requested a manual of my course to teach to others, I have written the following guide to practical self-defense for women. I hope it will help you learn the skills that can spare you mental and physical anguish, and possibly even save your life.

If you are the target of an attack, your life is in danger, and you must be able to defend yourself. Being mentally prepared enables you to react automatically and quickly so that you can escape.

Chapter I   Mental Preparedness

It is human nature to avoid thinking of unpleasant possibilities; we like to believe that "it will never happen to me." So it is possible that you have never asked yourself what you would do if you were attacked. Or perhaps you *have* thought about it and decided the best thing to do is just to go along with your attacker. *Submission to an attacker is no defense;* neither is it a guarantee that you will escape serious physical harm.

According to the U.S. Crime Index compiled by the F.B.I., violent crime in the United States has been steadily increasing. The number of reported offenses increased 9 percent from 1974 to 1975. Violent crimes, including murder, aggravated assault, and rape, increased 5 percent. From 1969 through 1974 violent crime has increased 47 percent, reflecting a 47 percent rise in the number of aggravated assaults, a 49 percent rise in the number of forcible rapes, and a 40 percent increase in the number of murders committed.[1]

According to the latest F.B.I. statistics, serious crimes occur at the rate of nineteen per minute. There is one instance of violent crime every thirty-three seconds; this includes an aggravated assault every seventy seconds, a forcible rape every ten minutes, and a murder every twenty-six minutes somewhere in the United States.[2]

Many of the statistics connected with rape in particular are surprising, because they are contrary to general beliefs. Some 34 percent of all rapes occur in the victim's own home. Almost 50 percent are committed by someone known to the victim. A large percentage of rapists are married and employed men; according to one study, 60 percent of rapists are married and lead normal sexual lives at home.[3] Finally, experts estimate that two to ten times as many rapes are committed as are ever reported.

Some women feel that self-defense techniques are mainly for single women; they think they are safe from attack because they are married or live with their families. This is not true. The advice in this book is for *all* women, since every woman is vulnerable *at some time,* whether in a park, a shopping center, a parking lot, or in her own home.

Some parts of this manual may mention circumstances that are different from your own—for example, you may not drive a car or live in an apartment. However, your circumstances can change; it is best to be aware of all of the possibilities of self-defense. All women, from junior high school age to senior citizens —single, married, or living with families —are vulnerable to attack, and they should be aware of this fact.

Probably the biggest problem women have in self-defense is an emotional one. Many women say, "I don't think I could really hurt anyone." They are not sure they could fight back and attempt to hurt their assailant in order to escape. Some women doubt their strength, others fear causing permanent injury. Part of the instruction is aimed at convincing them that submitting to an assailant because he has promised not to hurt them may not work.

The socially ingrained idea that women are passive and nonviolent increases this problem. Such beliefs can only be overcome by this thought: if you are the target of an attack, your life is in danger and you must be able to defend yourself. You have no guarantee that physical harm will not result even if you submit to sexual assault. Rape victims are sometimes murder victims as well, even when they were told that submission would keep them from being harmed. This reminder might help the person who thinks she couldn't react physically to see self-defense in a different light.

Women do not have to be natural fighters or aggressors in order to handle themselves physically and emotionally in self-defense. Think of it in its proper perspective. When threatened, you retaliate for your own preservation; and you may have only one chance. The best response to an attack is to react automatically and with skill in an attempt to get away. Women should be trained in escape methods so that these methods become an automatic response.

There is one school of thought that advises women to go along with an attacker, in hopes of being able to talk him out of raping or harming them. Another argument is that submission and compliance will "calm" the rapist, and that even if the woman is then raped, she will not be seriously injured. However, one study made in Denver supports the idea that the best strategy is to resist, and that the victim of an attempted attack should refuse to allow the attacker to intimidate her. The Denver study showed that the usual technique of the rapist involves locating women who are weak or vulnerable (such as the old, handicapped, or intoxicated), and making sure that the victim is alone and that the environment is safe, that is, a secluded lake shore or vacant lot. His next step is to make contact with his victim in order to intimidate her, whether by simply asking her for directions or a light, or by making an obscene comment or gesture. *If a woman refuses to be intimidated at this early stage, she is likely to be able to escape.* The rapist is looking for a frightened, submissive woman whom he can further intimidate into accompanying him or complying; he will usually threaten to kill or hurt her if she does not comply, and promises that if she submits, she will not be hurt.[4]

However, despite such promises, roughness occurs in 29 percent of all reported rapes, non-brutal beatings in 25 percent, brutal beatings in 20 percent and choking in 12 percent.[5] From clinical experiences with rapists and their victims, and studies of sex offenders in general, a pattern emerges showing that the rapist has usually planned the rape in advance, and that he is motivated not by sexual feelings, but by aggression, rage, and the wish to humiliate his victim.

Since most rapists are prepared and determined to commit rape, and have selected their victim in advance, there is little value in trying to "talk the rapist out of it." And, since most men do not expect a physical response from women, an immediate attack which involves the element of surprise can give a woman the upper hand in an attack situation, and give her enough time to get away.

Again, submitting to an attacker who has promised not to harm you is no defense, because you have no guarantee of safety. After he has committed the rape, the rapist may see his victim as a threat to him, since she may tell the police, and there may be a strong motivation to silence her.

Finally, you may not be able to think of a way to talk an attacker out of it; in most cases, attacks occur so quickly that women report feeling that they were frozen with fear. Your mind may not work in such a situation. However, if your muscles are trained to react automatically, and you use an effective escape technique, you may be able to get out of the situation.

You don't need to know every exercise in this manual to be able to defend yourself effectively. In an actual attack situation, you may remember only one thing —but that one thing can save your life. For example, one woman who had taken this self-defense course, when attacked on the street, remembered to try to hit her assailant in the face. A large ring that she was wearing caught him in the eye, and she was able to get away.

Each woman may find that she has a technique that works for her, or that feels comfortable; this is good, because it increases the chance that she will remember and be able to use that technique in an actual attack situation. Another woman who had been learning and practicing the snap-kick in self-defense class was attacked by two men. She immobilized one with a snap-kick to the groin, and his companion was startled enough to let her get away.

Some women may feel more comfortable carrying a nail file than keys; the important point is that you choose one or two methods that work for you and then consistently carry them out.

Of course, the best way to protect yourself is through preventive measures such as those given in chapter three. Taking the proper precautions—locking doors, avoiding parks and other secluded areas at night, exercising caution in parking lots, and so on—is the best insurance. Women who want to increase their awareness of the problem of attacks can attend movies that are shown by police and citizens' groups. They could join discussion groups or lobbying efforts, or organizations such as the Feminist Alliance Against Rape, or they could volunteer to work for a local rape crisis center.

At what age should self-defense be introduced? The answer to this rests completely on the maturity level of the individual rather than on her age. There are policies in some places that prohibit teaching this type of program to persons under eighteen years of age. This reflects a very shortsighted attitude. Teenagers are just as vulnerable to attack as mature women, if not more so, since they spend a great amount of time going to and from school functions, dates, places of employment, and many other destinations either alone or in the company of others their age. One study found that girls between the ages of fifteen and nineteen accounted for one fourth of all reported rapes. Another found that students comprise 27 percent of all rape victims and "made up the largest group having stated occupations."[6]

If a teacher takes the time to explain the seriousness of the self-defense classes, most students will be eager to learn and will accept the teaching in the right frame of mind. It may *not* be worthwhile to teach the self-defense methods in this manual before junior high school. Elementary school children may not understand that these techniques are not to be used on annoying brothers and sisters or for showing off to friends. As with any serious sport or discipline, self-defense tactics can be dangerous if practiced at inappropriate times and places, and either the "victim" or the "attacker" may be injured. Even on the junior and senior high school level, students should be reminded that self-defense is not to be used outside of a controlled practice situation, except if needed to ward off an attack.

Children should, of course, be taught to recognize and run from potentially dangerous situations. Some rules apply equally to adults, teenagers, and children, such as never accepting food or rides from strangers, not approaching cars too closely if asked for directions, going to a well-lighted area, house, or store if they are being followed, and so on. Young boys as well as girls are subject to attack, and should be warned and told how to respond to a dangerous situation. The police and other agencies often present programs in the schools that teach children how to recognize and react to trouble.

---

[1] F.B.I. Uniform Crime Report, 1974.
[2] *Ibid.*
[3] Amir, Menachem, Patterns in Forcible Rape. University of Chicago Press. Chicago, 1971.
[4] *Psychology Today,* January 1975.
[5] Amir.
[6] Amir, and Brown, Brenda S. "Crime Against Women Alone." A System of Analysis of the Memphis Police Department Sex Crime Squad's 1973 Rape Investigation, May 18, 1974.

Chapter II What Is Self-Defense?

Self-defense is a means of self-preservation that uses weaponless combat to ward off an attacker. It is not a sport like judo, karate, or aikido, but a combination of many techniques taken from these and other areas, such as jujitsu and even street fighting. A woman who is experienced in methods of self-defense can use her arms and legs as four separate weapons, making it extremely difficult for an attacker to anticipate or retaliate against more than one or two limbs at a time.

Remember that self-defense is defined by its name: it is a way to defend yourself from a dangerous situation in order to escape. Runnning away from danger is by far the best solution. But if you are unable to run, being skilled in the art of self-defense will help you escape from the danger of unavoidable physical contact.

Self-defense also involves teaching women to defend themselves *legally*. There are cases in the courts today in which women who shot or stabbed men who assaulted them — even in their own homes — have been prosecuted, and even convicted. Knives and guns and, in many states, Mace, cannot legally be used against anyone. Also, the fists or arms and legs of boxers and persons who are extremely skilled in the martial arts are considered weapons that can be used illegally.

However, if you are not a martial arts expert and you defend yourself physically with your arms and legs, or with keys, a nail file, or a squeeze lemon, it is obvious that you are only defending yourself in order to get away. Also, there is less likelihood that any of these "weapons" will be taken and used against you, as can happen with guns, knives and Mace.

Experts in the martial arts usually consider them to be sports, rather than a means of protection. One man with a third-degree black belt in judo stated that if he encountered trouble on the street, he would run rather than use his knowledge of judo against an attacker. It is always better to avoid physical contact if at all possible. Persons in the martial arts learn temper control along with their skills, since they are taught that these techniques should never be used in anger or to "try out" what they have learned.

There is no such thing as instant self-defense; it must be practiced continually in order to become automatic and, in turn, effective. Timing is extremely important in the success of an escape; therefore, the technique must become automatic through practice. There can be no stopping in the middle of a technique, for a moment's hesitation will give the assailant time to recover from the shock of an apparently trained resistance.

Since the general makeup of self-defense includes various techniques taken from judo, karate, aikido, jujitsu, and street fighting, it may be helpful to understand the backgrounds of these techniques, known as the weaponless arts of fighting.

Jujitsu was developed by Japanese warriors who had to fight bare-handed, long before bows and arrows or firearms were used in warfare. Prison guards also needed methods of controlling prisoners without fatally harming them. Schools of this art sprang up in Japan, and though they differed in name, the subject matter was almost identical. Techniques of chopping, poking, kicking with the heel and ball of the foot, and bending and twisting of the joints were studied and practiced until an unarmed person could overcome his or her assailant with ease and effectiveness. Some of these schools, however, practiced dangerous and violent techniques which resulted in a poor image for the school and often the art itself. These schools were usually poorly supervised and had a high rate of injury.

Judo (ju-gentle, do-way) evolved from jujitsu through Professor Jigoro Kano. His school, the Kodokan School of Judo, was established in 1882. Dr. Kano added his own methods to some of its tactics in order to create a discipline combining intellectual and physical capacity. As a result, a great rivalry developed between the Kodokan School of Judo and the Jujitsu School. A tournament was held with fifteen contestants from each school. The Kodokan School won thirteen of these contests, and the remaining two resulted in draws. This provided the necessary impetus to establish Kodokan Judo as the superior school in techniques and principles.

Karate originated in China and consists principally of hand and foot blows. It is often confused with judo, which consists of throwing, choking, arm bars, and mat techniques, while chops and kicks are not allowed. Karate is a Japanese word meaning "empty unarmed hand" and is similar to judo only in the fact that both are weaponless means of combat. Karate blows are aimed at parts of the body that are easily injured, such as the stomach and the throat. A karate blow can cripple and even kill. In practice and competition, karate experts stop short of hitting each other, or they touch their opponent lightly.

There are four major types of karate—Chinese, Japanese, Korean, and Okinawan. All use the same basic techniques, but each stresses different skills and has its own characteristic style of movement. For example, Korean karate, called tae kwon do, emphasizes kicking. Chinese karate, called kung fu, uses a flowing, circular motion that differs from the hard, powerful movements of the other types.

Becoming proficient in judo or karate is a very time-consuming task. Any school that advertises fast methods of acquiring these skills should be avoided. An instructor's ability and training can be determined by the color belt worn with the *gi* (uniform). Higher ranking belts are awarded for successful competition in judo and karate tournaments. The black belt is the highest rank in both sports.

Aikido is a technique made up of stylized holds and locks that include bending and twisting and the application of pressure against joints to cause pain, immobilization, and fractures. The holds and

What Is Self-Defense?

locks in aikido have been known for hundreds of years, but the movements themselves are fairly recent. The art of aikido itself takes years to master, and its artists are interested in style, beauty, agility, and precision. In self-defense we use the same basic holds and locks for twisting, bending, and applying pressure but without the aikido stylization. Practical self-defense means practical and simple methods that can be easily learned and applied within a short amount of time.

Judo and karate are acceptable ways of learning self-defense techniques for those who are willing to spend the time and money on the extensive training necessary. However, before signing up for lessons, the credibility of the establishment and the qualifications of its instructors should be thoroughly checked out. Any place that advertises fast methods of learning these sports should be avoided. The mastery of sports like judo and karate takes a great deal of time and energy. Thus, for women who want to learn practical self-defense techniques that are easily mastered, judo or karate is not the answer.

Also, women often find that in any kind of self-defense or martial arts program taught by men, the instructors are not really sensitive to women's fears. In addition, some male instructors build false security and confidence by "taking a dive" in self-defense lessons, thereby leading women to believe that the techniques are much simpler than they really are.

There is a real need for self-defense programs designed specifically for women, using effective and practical methods that can be learned quickly. These programs should be taught by women whenever possible. The self-defense techniques in this manual can even be self-taught, although you will need a partner with whom to practice the more advanced techniques.

Your practice partner can be a member of your family, a friend or a neighbor—anyone who is available and interested in learning the techniques with you. It is best if your practice partner is a woman. Practicing with a man is apt to be discouraging because a man will want to use all his strength in the holds, and you will probably not be able to break them. All of the techniques in this manual depend to a great extent on the element of surprise and on speed and agility used to combat strength. Therefore, if you practice with someone of your own size who is also learning, you will be able to work up to the quickness necessary to combat someone of greater strength.

Always keep in mind when you are practicing these techniques that self-defense is serious business, and practice should be approached with the proper mental attitude. You should be relaxed but serious. While learning and practicing self-defense techniques is very satisfying to individuals, it is not just for fun. Practice sessions should not become just playful "horsing around."

I have never had a serious injury occur in my classes. If you are careful, use mats, learn the correct way to fall so that you will not be hurt (chapter VI), and have clear signals between you and your partner, there should be little chance of accidental injury. Warm-up exercises will help to tone the muscles

What Is Self-Defense?

and will reduce the possibility of a sprain or other injury. Also, a program of exercises will help to condition you so that, if you are attacked, you will be better able to run.

The following exercise routine can be used as a model. Other exercises may be used in place of any one of these: the important thing is to encourage flexibility by doing the bending and stretching exercises set out below.

In this series of exercises, you start with the head and work your way down to the feet.

STANDING

1. **Head rotations.** Bring your chin down toward your chest, letting your head hang. Rotate your head in a complete circle, twice to the right and twice to the left.

2. **Shoulder shrugs and rotations.** Shrug the shoulders up and down several times. Rotate the shoulders forward five times and backward five times.

3. **Arm circles.** Arms should be held straight out to the sides, at shoulder level. Move arms and hands in small circles forward, increasing the size of the circles. Repeat, going in the opposite direction.

4. **Side stretches to the left and right.** Without bending forward at the waist, bring your right arm over your head when stretching left, and vice versa when stretching right.

5. **Waist stretch.** Bend over and touch the floor with your hands. Your knees can be slightly bent. Come up to a standing position, put hands on hips and lean backward.

6. **Hip rotation.** With hands on hips, rotate hips in a circle, keeping your upper body and feet in place. Circle hips to the left twice and then twice to the right.

7. **Side lunges.** For thighs. With feet apart, lunge from side to side, bending the knee of your right leg as your hips lunge right, and vice versa. Your feet should stay flat on the floor.

SIT ON FLOOR

8. **Leg stretch.** With legs apart, stretch your head down to your left knee, then to your right knee. Stretch straight out to the center. Use slow static stretches instead of bouncing.

STANDING

9. **Running in place.** Finish by running in place for a minute or two.

Chapter III Prevention And Preparedness

Preventive measures should be practiced in an attempt to discourage an assailant or intruder and make you a less likely target. Develop a sense of awareness that becomes a part of your life style. Maintain these habits at all times: a false sense of security because you feel you know an area or neighborhood can cause you to let your defenses down and be careless. If you lock your car everywhere else, why not in your own driveway? You have no guarantee that you will never have a problem where you have always felt safe.

Below are some suggestions that will help to increase your awareness of situations that could occur and help you to prevent them. Again, some of the circumstances described here may not apply to you at this time; however, it cannot hurt you to be aware of them.

Remember that prevention is your best and most effective means of avoiding attack. If you are alert and follow the suggestions outlined below, you will be much less likely to become the victim of an attack.

AT HOME

1. Install a peephole in the door so you can see who is outside without opening the door.

2. Make sure there is a secure lock on all exterior doors. Chain locks will not stop anyone who is serious about getting into your home.

3. Replace locks when you move to a new house or apartment. You have no guarantee that a key to the old lock was not kept.

4. Make sure all windows have locks, and use them. In basement or first floor apartments, bars on the windows are the best security.

5. Don't leave your door unlocked and your apartment empty even for a few minutes, while carrying in groceries, checking laundry, taking out garbage, and so on.

6. All windows should have curtains or blinds drawn after dark. Never undress in front of a window.

7. Ask service repairmen to slide identification under the door, and never admit one without knowing he was expected.

8. Use your first initial on the mail box and in the phone book.

9. Don't advertise the fact that you live alone or with another woman.

Prevention and Preparedness

ON FOOT

1. When returning home or to your car, have your key ready. Put heavy tape on the key to make it easy to find among the others.

2. Be cautious of infrequently used elevators or service elevators, especially during nonworking hours. Parking ramp and basement parking elevators also warrant caution, especially late at night or early in the morning.

3. Don't hitchhike or accept rides with strangers. Once in the car you may find that the inside door handle has been removed.

4. Be leery of people seeking directions, and keep your distance from the car.

5. If you are being followed by a car, turn around and walk the other way. If possible, go up a one-way street. License numbers, if you can get them, should be reported as soon as possible.

6. If you must walk in a questionable area, get a friend to walk with you.

7. Be alert to what is happening around you. Take notice of people as well as hidden areas such as doorways, bushes, alleys, and parked cars, and stay a safe distance away from such areas.

8. Maintain a steady pace and know where you are going. A confident, alert posture in itself can discourage attackers.

9. Be prepared mentally as well as physically for any type of action.

10. Do not get weighed down with packages or allow them to block your vision.

11. A large purse sticking out is like a neon sign. Keep your purse tucked under your arm.

12. Remember that your best defense is to run. If you anticipate having to walk somewhere at night or in a sparsely populated area during the day, the clothes you wear should not inhibit your ability to run.

13. Certain types of shoes are hard to run in, such as sandals, clogs, and platforms. If you can get them off in a hurry, running becomes much easier.

14. Don't wear chains, medallions, or necklaces that could be used to choke you. Whistles on chains around the wrist work well, but never around the neck.

15. Footsteps in pace with your own can be checked by changing your

Prevention and Preparedness

pace several times. If they persist, head for a well-lighted area if possible. If the person is not within striking or choking distance, yell "Fire!" or scream as loudly as possible. Try to get into a store or to a house with lights on.

16. If you must wait for a bus or a ride, don't lean against a tree or a pole, against which you could easily be pinned. Keep your hands out of your pockets and your feet apart; you do not have good balance for escaping from a dangerous situation with your feet together and/or hands in your pockets. You must be ready for a situation and not give an assailant a head start by being off balance.

IN YOUR CAR

1. Lock your car after getting into as well as out of it. You could very easily pick up an unwanted passenger at a red light if your doors are not locked while driving.

2. Even when returning to a locked car, check the back seat and the floor before getting in. A locked car is not that much of a challenge to someone who wants to get in badly enough.

3. When you leave your car to be serviced or parked, take your house key off the key ring. You would never know if it had been copied until it was too late. Papers in the glove compartment often have the address that the key will fit.

4. If someone attempts to get into your car at a red light or a stop sign, blow your car horn and keep your window rolled up. It is also much easier to get away if you leave your car in gear.

5. Don't pick up hitchhikers.

6. If you pass a driver in distress, stay in your car and report it to the police or nearest service station.

7. If you have car trouble, raise the hood and get back inside the car. Keep the doors locked and windows rolled up. If a stranger stops, ask him to report your car to the police or nearest service station.

8. Valuable items should be kept out of sight.

9. If stopped by a policeman or sheriff in an unmarked car, ask for identification before rolling your window down all the way. Even those in marked cars should be willing to show you identification.

Prevention and Preparedness

IF YOU MUST BE HOME ALONE

1. If your life-style requires living alone or being alone for long periods of time, have a dog.

2. Obscene phone calls should be reported to the police immediately. Either stay with a friend or have one stay with you until the police can be of some assistance to you.

3. Do not answer calls for your husband or roommate by giving information about where he or she is or when he or she will be back.

4. Try to give the impression to a caller or person at the door that you are not alone.

5. Keep the garage door locked at all times to avoid easy access to your home or the floor of your car.

6. Have a neighbor call every night to make sure you are all right and that things are secure.

7. Become proficient enough in judo, karate, or self-defense to protect yourself.

DEFENSIVE MEASURES

There are many legal items you can carry on the street that are practical, but they will not help you unless they are in your hand ready to use. Your main reason for carrying any such item is to surprise an assailant long enough to run to safety, because he will not be expecting any preparedness on your part. However, be sure to check out the item you intend to carry to make sure it will work if needed.

1. A plastic lemon filled with juice can squirt up to several feet away. You should check to see that it is full and will squirt when pressed. Then carry it with the cap off and, in the event of a dangerous situation, squirt it at the assailant. The eyes are the best area to disable in order to escape, and the lemon juice produces a momentary blindness that could enable you to get away.

2. Another practical item which most people already carry is a set of keys. These can be placed in the hand with the keys protruding out between the fingers and used in a manner similar to brass knuckles. Be sure to hold the keys firmly, and once again the best target is the facial area, especially the eyes.

3. A lighted cigarette put to someone's face can provide the few seconds necessary to get away.

Prevention and Preparedness

4. A roll of pennies carried in your hand can add a lot of force to a blow. If you can punch your hand up under the assailant's nose it will cause instant tears.

5. A ball point pen in hand with the cartridge down can do a lot of damage if used in or near the eyes.

6. Rings can scratch the face or eyes and cause them to water.

7. A hat pin carried in your hand can be used to earn the few seconds needed for escape.

8. A nail file is easily concealed in a woman's hand and can be used effectively in the face.

The above methods might sound gruesome, but if your life is being threatened, you must use any means possible to get away. Your best escape is one that is premeditated. If you have thought through the situation beforehand, and even practiced the motions necessary, you will be much more likely to be able to react effectively, and not freeze or panic.

Chapter IV Pressure Points And Vulnerable Areas

Pressure points and vulnerable areas of the body are the targets of our self-defense attacks. We have two objectives in mind: surprising and physically distracting the assailant. If you are able to poke the attacker in the eye you have achieved the surprise element. If he is wearing glasses, tear them off. You have probably been poked in the eye before, so you are aware of how quickly they water. Poking a finger in the eye of an assailant may sound horrible but it is very effective in causing watering and allowing you to escape.

The second objective of physically distracting the assailant is used if you are in a more confining hold, for example, if both your arms are immobilized. In that situation you could bring a knee very sharply into the groin area, making the assailant loosen his hold and allowing you to free yourself and get away.

Once again, if there is any way to avoid physical contact, it is far better than confrontation. A woman is not likely to be as strong as her attacker, and escape may not be successful if mere strength is relied upon. Therefore, the vulnerable areas should be well in mind and should be the target of any escape attempt.

Hardly anyone thinks of the ears as being vulnerable, but they are extremely accessible to a victim. By cupping your hands and delivering a swift blow to the ears you can create a shock wave to the brain which can cause passing out and

Fig. 1

Pressure Points And Vulnerable Areas

possibly even death. Figure 1 illustrates the cupped position of the hands coming in towards the attacker's ears. Figure 2 shows the swiftness with which the hands are withdrawn after delivering the blow. Remember that in order to be effective, this must be a whiplike action from start to finish.

A less severe method that also uses the ears is to insert the thumbs into the indentations below the ear lobes and to push inward and upward simultaneously, keeping thumbs and wrists firm. This can be done either from the front or from behind, as illustrated in figure 3.

The nose may be attacked by shoving the heel of the hand vigorously underneath, causing the eyes to water and possibly damage to the cartilage of the nose. You may also use your hand as a blade and deliver a forceful blow across the bridge of the nose. Here you must be sure to use the fleshy side of your hand below the knuckle of the little finger, and not the finger itself. For best results the blow must be as forceful as possible.

Fig. 2 Fig. 3

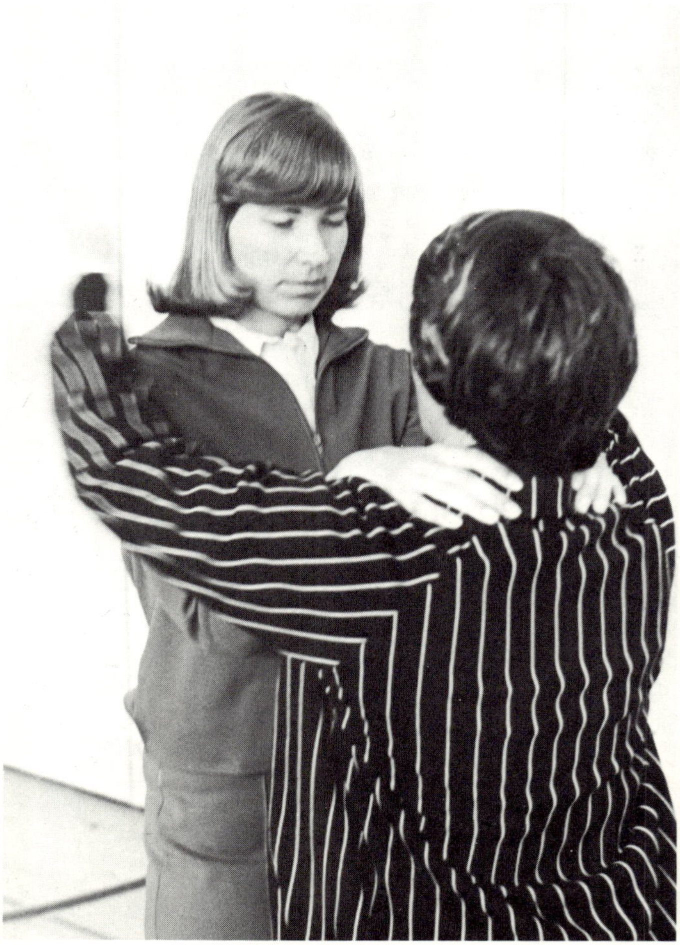

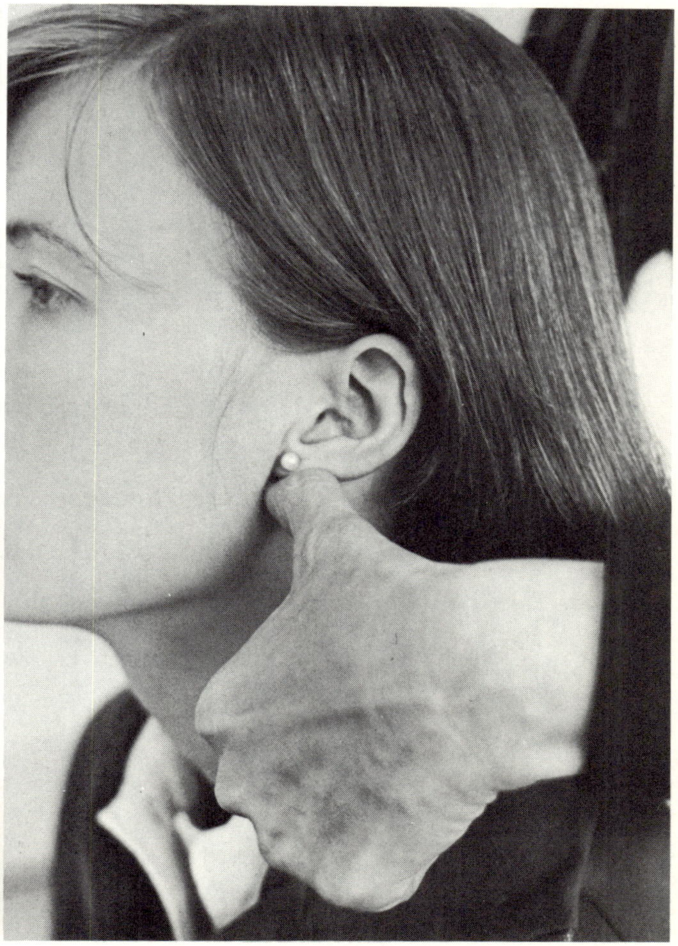

Pressure Points And Vulnerable Areas

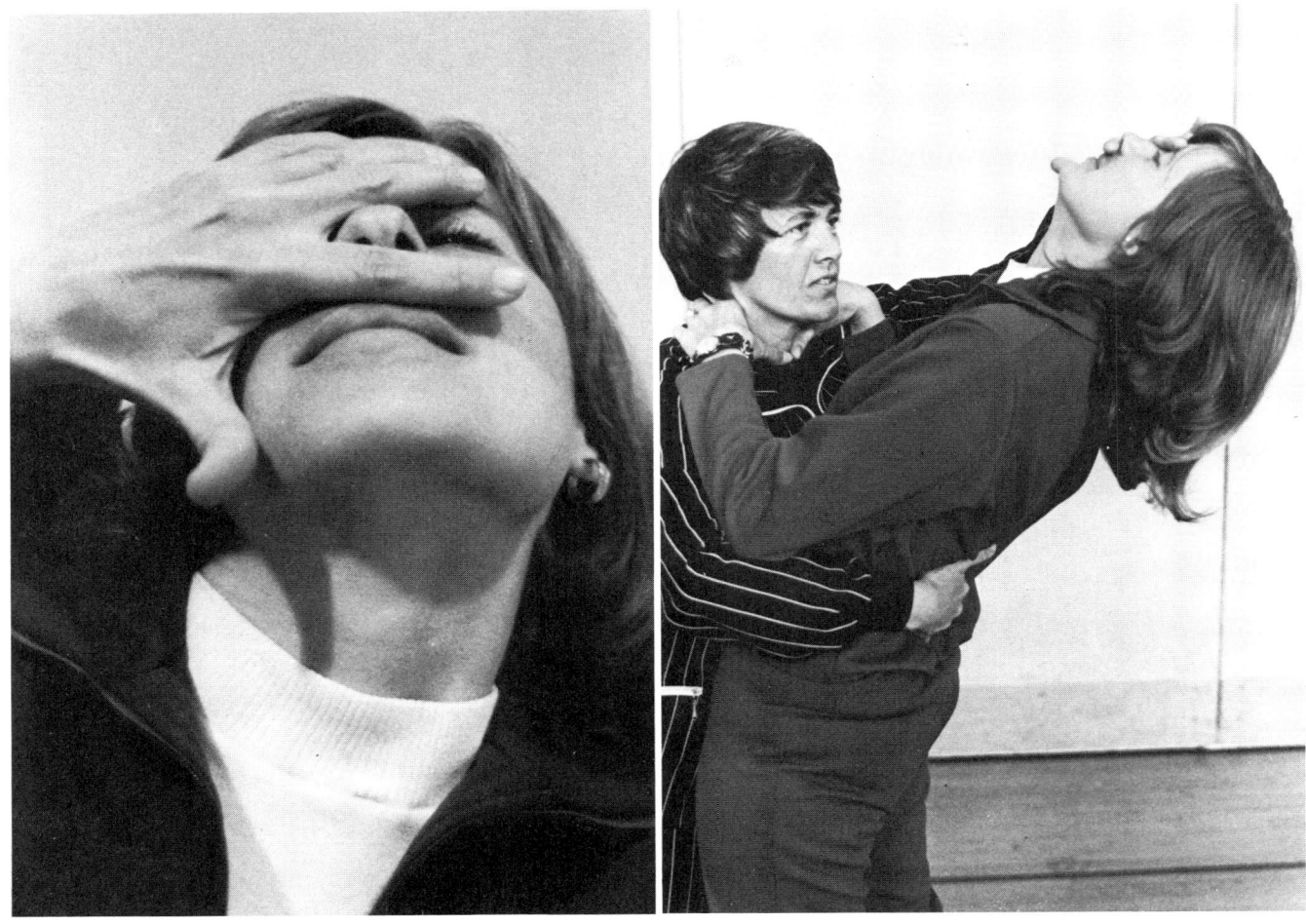

Fig. 4   Fig. 5

Another technique which is a favorite of mine has two distinct methods of delivery. The first is from a face to face position:

1. Slide the index finger under the nose cartilage.

2. Place the middle finger over the bridge of the nose, figure 4.

3. Use the other arm as a brace around the assailant's back.

4. Pushing up under the nose, use the brace arm to pull the assailant toward you, figure 5.

5. At the same time, this makes the groin area very vulnerable to a sharp blow with the knee.

Pressure Points And Vulnerable Areas

Fig. 6   Fig. 7

The second method is initiated from a side position with the assailant holding you in a head lock:

1. Using the arm closest to the assailant, reach up behind his nearest shoulder.

2. Place your index finger under his nose and your middle finger over the bridge of the nose, figure 6.

3. Pull the assailant's head back, bending him over your knee; the groin area then becomes vulnerable to a sharp blow with the free arm, figure 7.

Pressure Points And Vulnerable Areas

Fig. 8

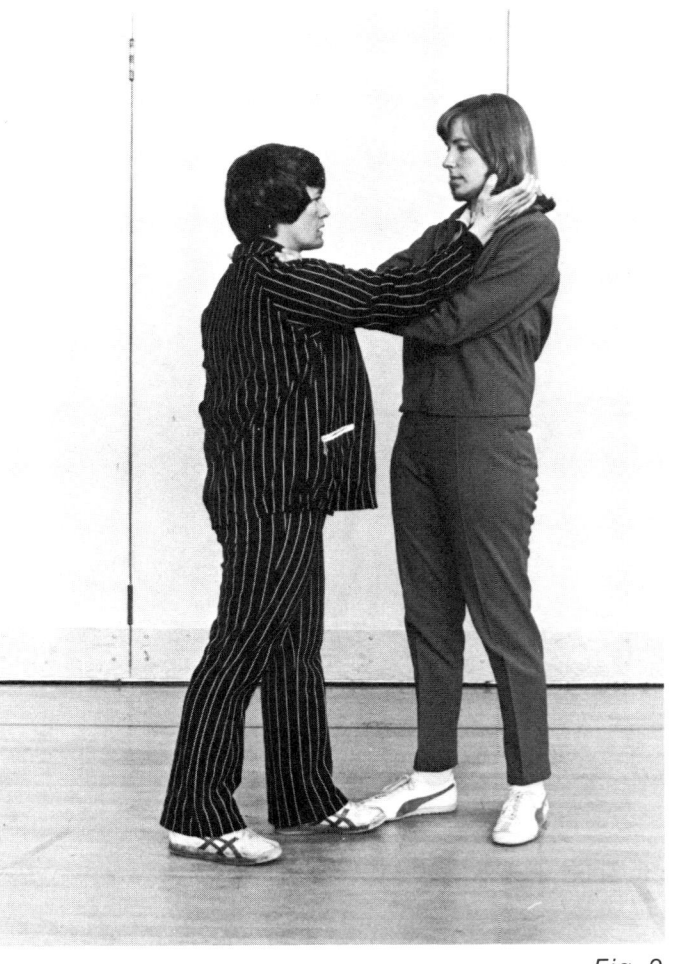
Fig. 9

The Adam's apple can also be the target of a forceful blow with either the knuckles or the fleshy side of the hand, figure 8. The blow must be a quick, whiplike strike.

The collar bone (or clavicle) can easily be broken with a sharp blow using the fleshy side of the hand. It is not a very thick bone, and some karate classes concentrate on the vulnerability of this area by having the students break one-inch pine boards. This can easily be accomplished with practice, and simulates the action of the blow and reaction of the collar bone, figure 9. The fleshy part of the side of the hand below the knuckles is very strong. In karate, continuous practice builds up a callous so blows can be harder; however, even without such training, you can direct a stunning or disabling blow at your attacker.

Pressure Points And Vulnerable Areas

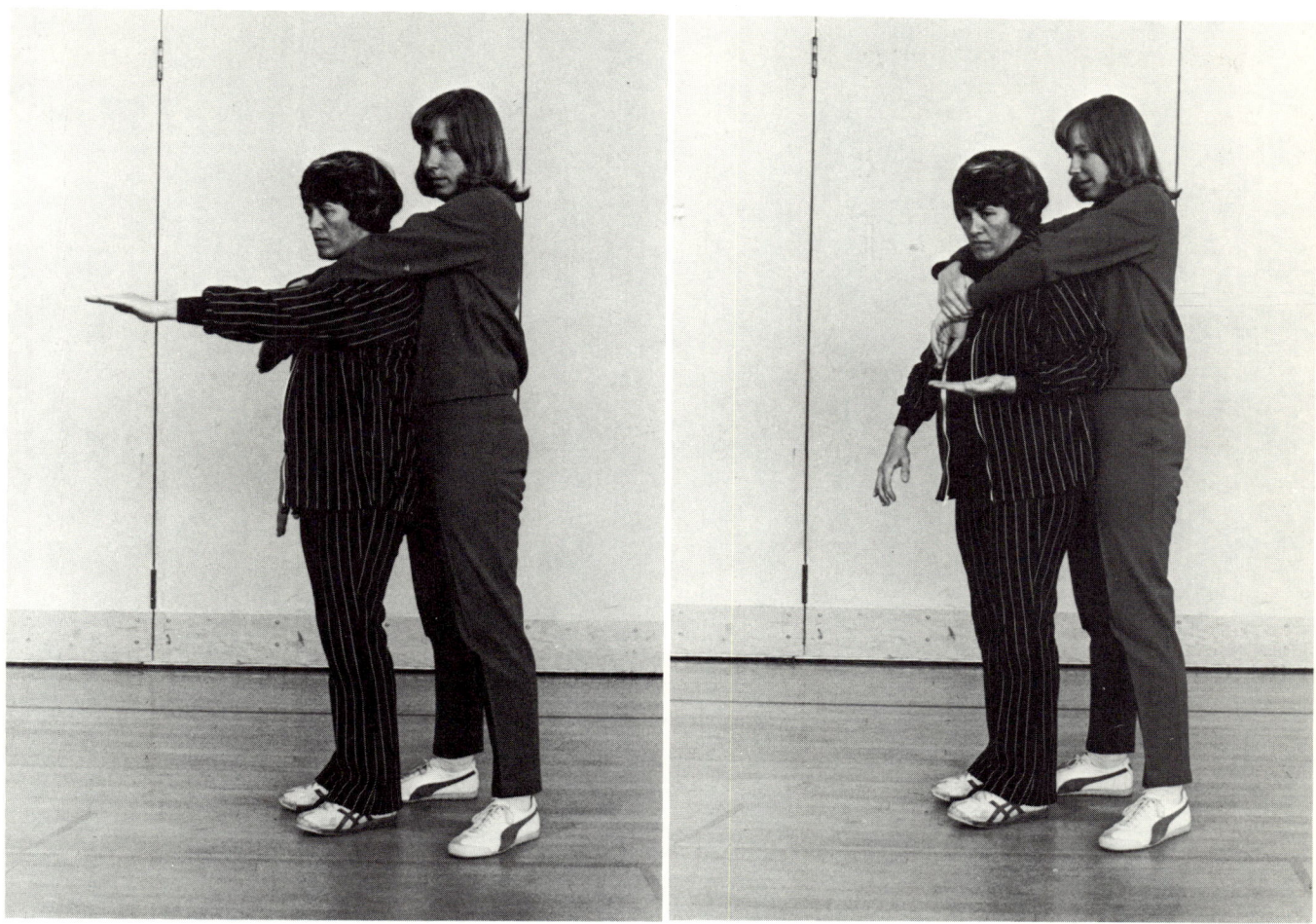

Fig. 10 Fig. 11

The pit of the stomach, or solar plexis, is the target for direct blows of the elbow:

1. Start with your arm out in front of you, palm down, figure 10.

2. As you move your arm back towards the target, rotate your palm upward, figure 11.

3. On contact your palm should be completely rotated to an upward position. This rotation of the forearm allows more momentum in the delivery of the blow, making the blow more forceful.

The groin area may be attacked by bringing the knee up underneath and into the groin as hard as possible. If he starts to protect the area and you cannot connect, go for another area such as the eyes, nose, or ears. If you are standing back farther from the assailant a well-placed snap-kick to the groin is a good technique for practical purposes (see chapter V).

The lateral cartilage of the knee can be

Pressure Points And Vulnerable Areas

Fig. 12   Fig. 13

damaged by a hard kick or stomp with your foot, figure 12, making it harder for your assailant to chase you once you have gotten away.

The foot also has many small bones that can be broken by stomping down hard with your heel. This can also be accomplished by bringing your knee up, pointing your toes up and heel down, and then kicking backwards into the assailant's shin, figure 13.

Chapter V   Escape Techniques

Although escape techniques may seem easy to do, they must be practiced until they become automatic if they are to work in a real situation. Practice partners should use loose grips until the whole sequence of the technique has been learned; then grips can be tightened, and techniques practiced with different partners.

Before getting into the actual practice of escape techniques, it is important to have safety signals which your partner will recognize. Such signals can be (1) simply yelling "stop!", (2) slapping your thigh three times, or (3) quickly stomping your foot three times. Everyone has a different level of pain, and therefore a simple signal is necessary to stop the technique when that level is reached in practice.

All escape techniques must have diversion, speed, and the element of surprise. They may possibly also need a follow-up, such as a snap-kick, forceful blow, or similar move.

Fig. 14

ESCAPE #1: ONE HAND EACH WRIST GRIP

If the assailant grabs both your wrists, figure 14, you can escape using the following method:

Escape Techniques

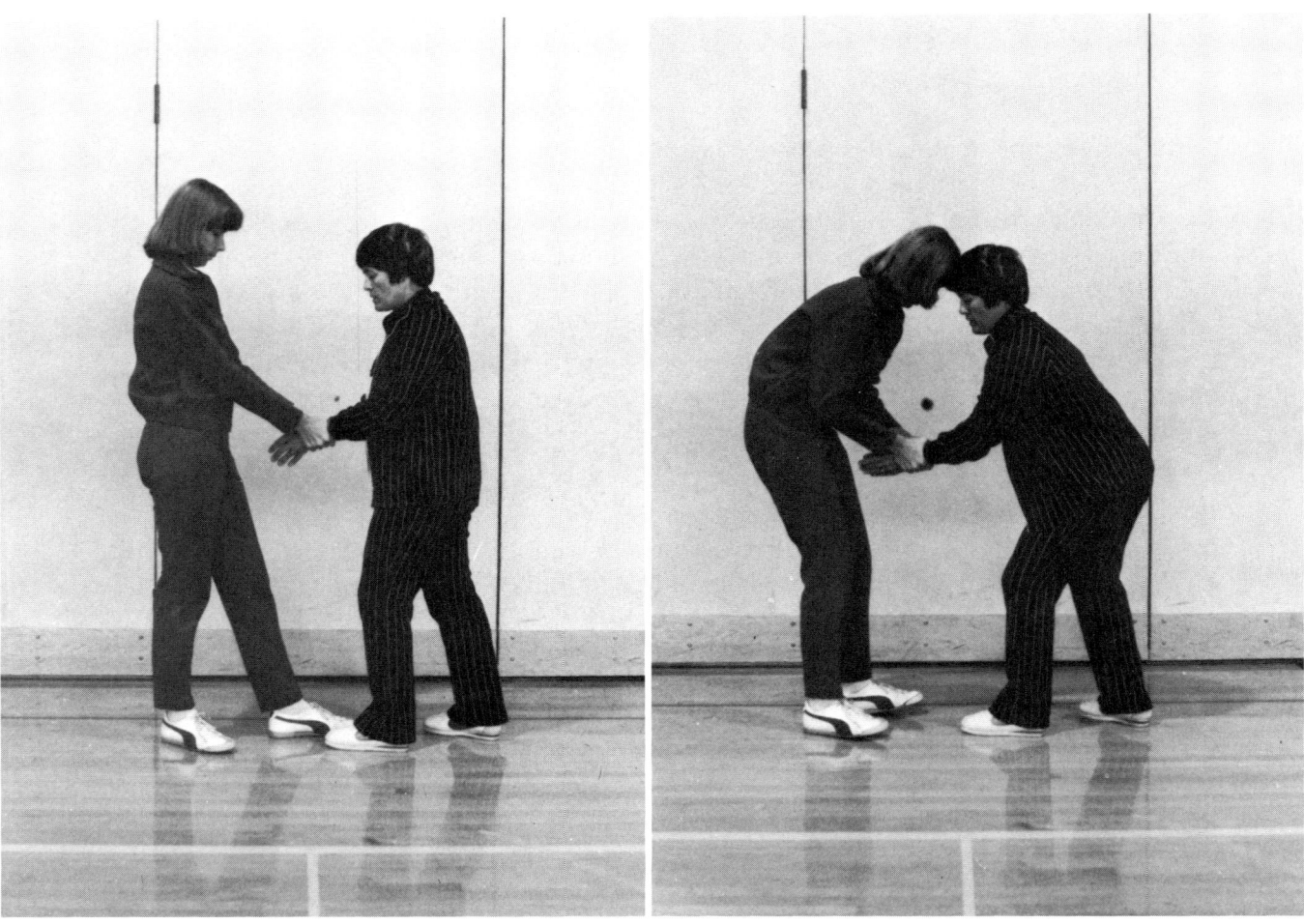

Fig. 15   Fig. 16

1. DIVERSION: Attempt to loosen up the assailant with a thrusting motion of the hands toward the groin area, figures 15 and 16.

2. Continue with the motion until you get an opposite reaction, such as the assailant attempting to move backwards to protect the area.

3. Quickly pull your hands back towards your body, turning your hands outward and upward until palms are facing up, figure 17 and 18.

4. When palms are in this position, snap outward with the thumbs leading, figure 19.

5. You must also use your legs to take a large step backwards as you work your arms back towards your body. This elongates the assailant's biceps muscles and makes them weaker, figures 20 and 21.

Escape Techniques

Fig. 17

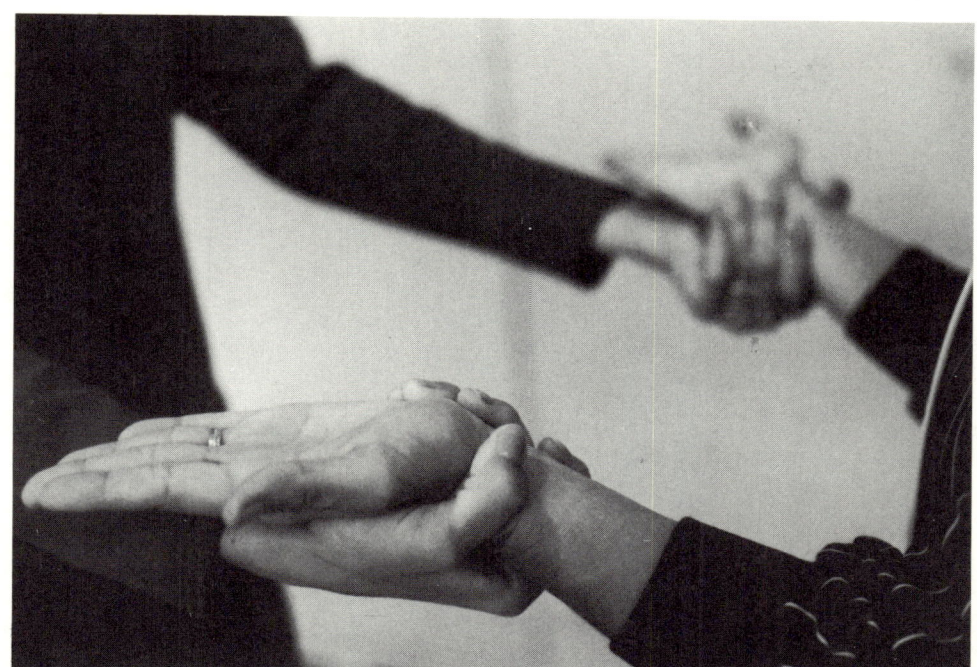

Fig. 19

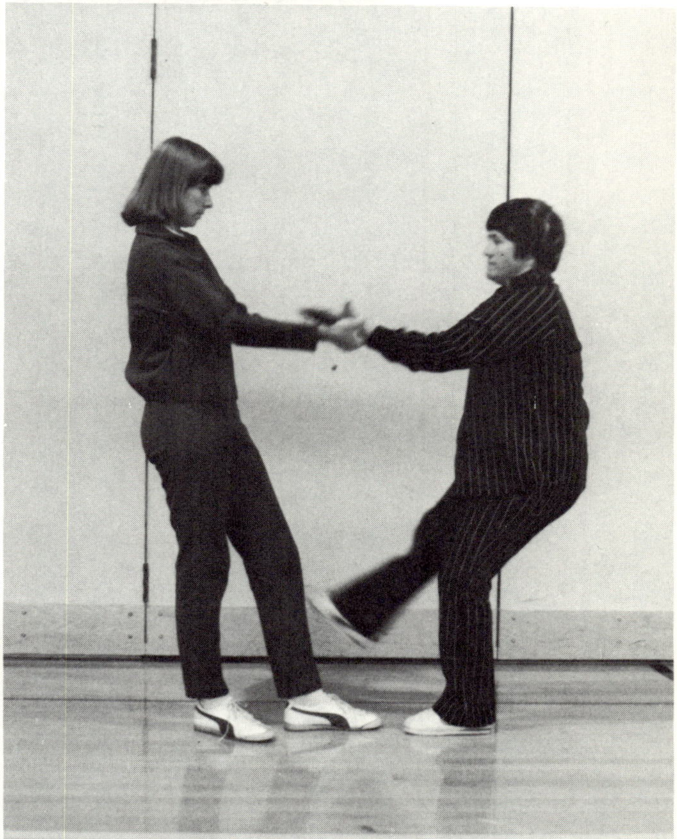

Fig. 18

Escape Techniques

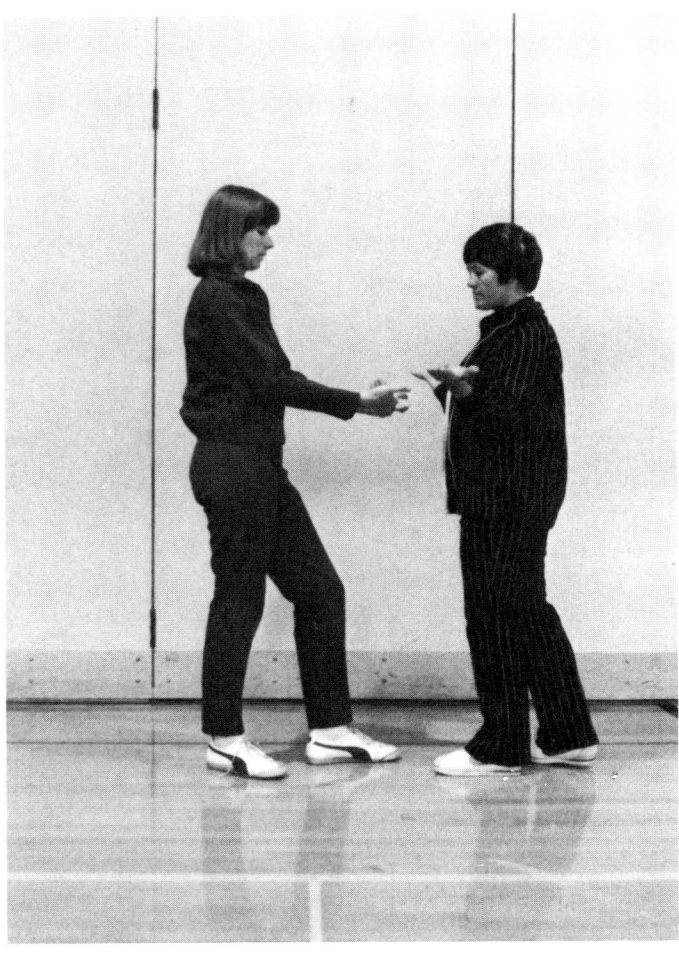

Fig. 20

Remember that this technique relies on speed and that there cannot be any hesitation. The reason this technique works is that you are continually turning your arms against the weakest part of the attacker's hands, his thumbs.

Common Faults:

- *Hesitation—technique not applied as one smooth move.*
- *Forgetting to first apply the diversion.*
- *The victim lifts her arms up instead of twisting out to the sides.*
- *The victim forgets to take a large step backwards while applying technique.*

Escape Techniques

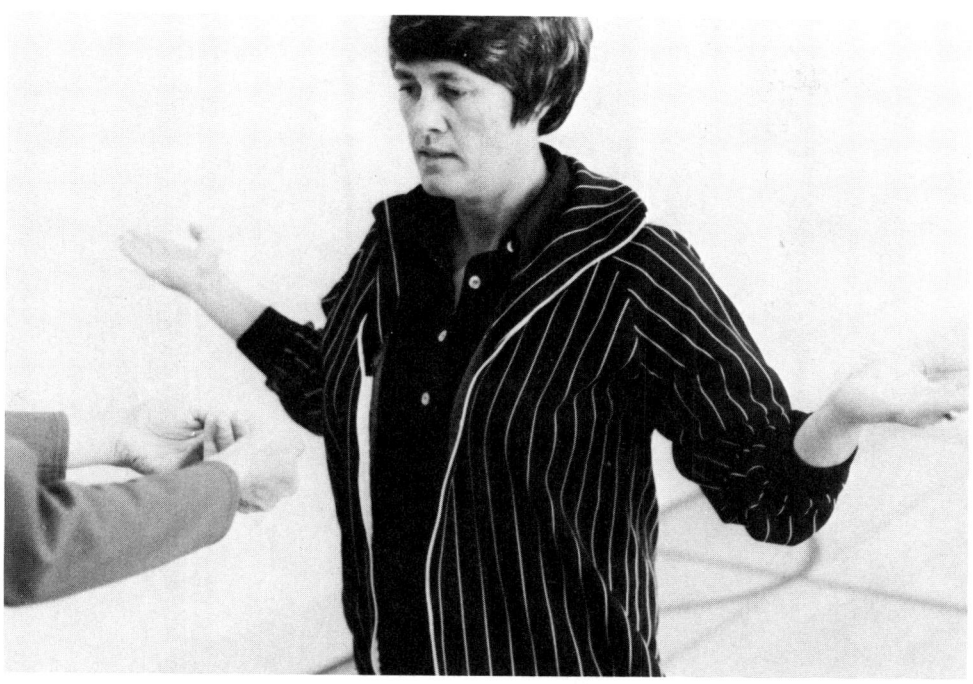

Fig. 21

If the opponent is holding on tightly, his momentum will carry him toward you as a result of your pulling backwards. This closeness may necessitate the application of another technique such as a chop under the nose cartilage or cupped hands over the ears before you are able to turn and run.

Escape Techniques

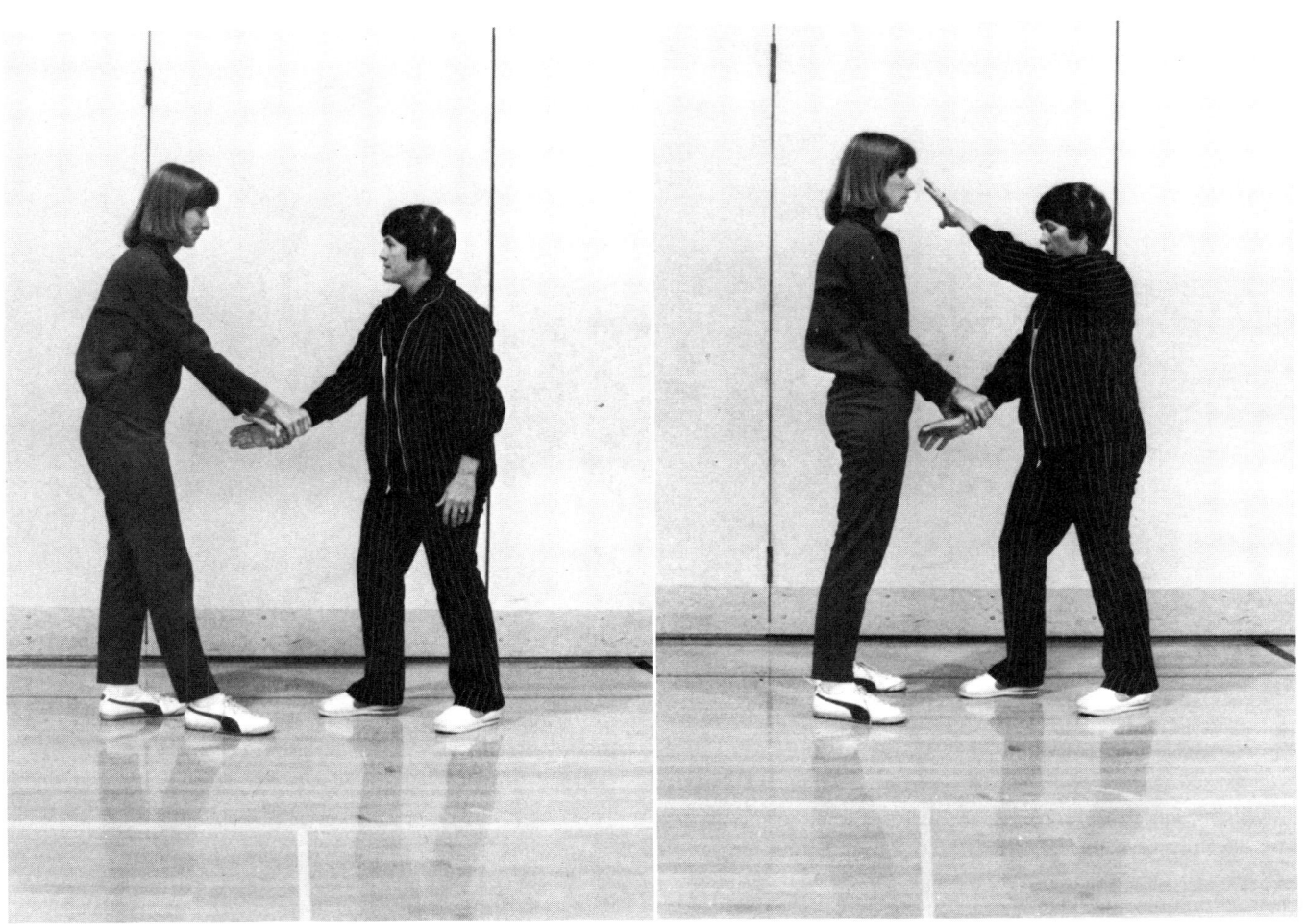

Fig. 22   Fig. 23

ESCAPE #2: TWO HANDS ON ONE WRIST, LOWER POSITION (Fig. 22)

1. DIVERSION: Use your free hand to thrust toward the groin area or face, figure 23.

2. Reach down through the opponent's arms, grasping the hand of your held wrist, figure 24.

3. Pull upward and outward while stepping away to the side (with the leg opposite the arm being held), thus elongating the attacker's biceps, figure 25.

Escape Techniques

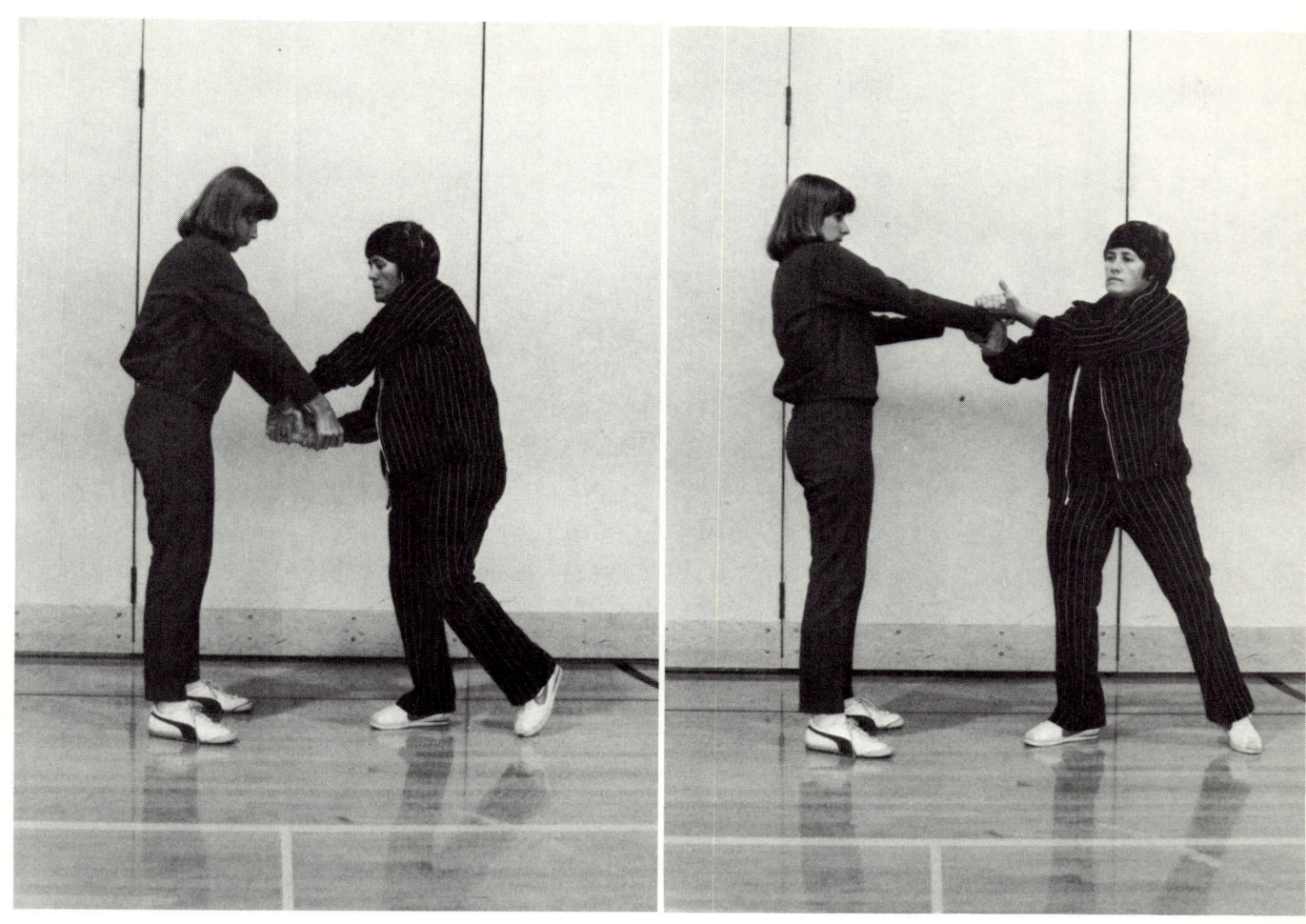

Fig. 24   Fig. 25

Common Faults:

- *Forgetting to apply the diversion.*
- *Gripping your fingers instead of the palm area of your hand for escape.*
- *Forgetting to step to the side to elongate and weaken biceps of attacker.*
- *Forgetting to pull up on your own hand after gripping palm.*

Once again you will probably need to follow up with a chop to the nose cartilage or other technique, since the assailant will be close to you. The hand you have freed will be more effective for this since it is much closer to the attacker. Be sure to practice this technique with both hands!

33

Escape Techniques

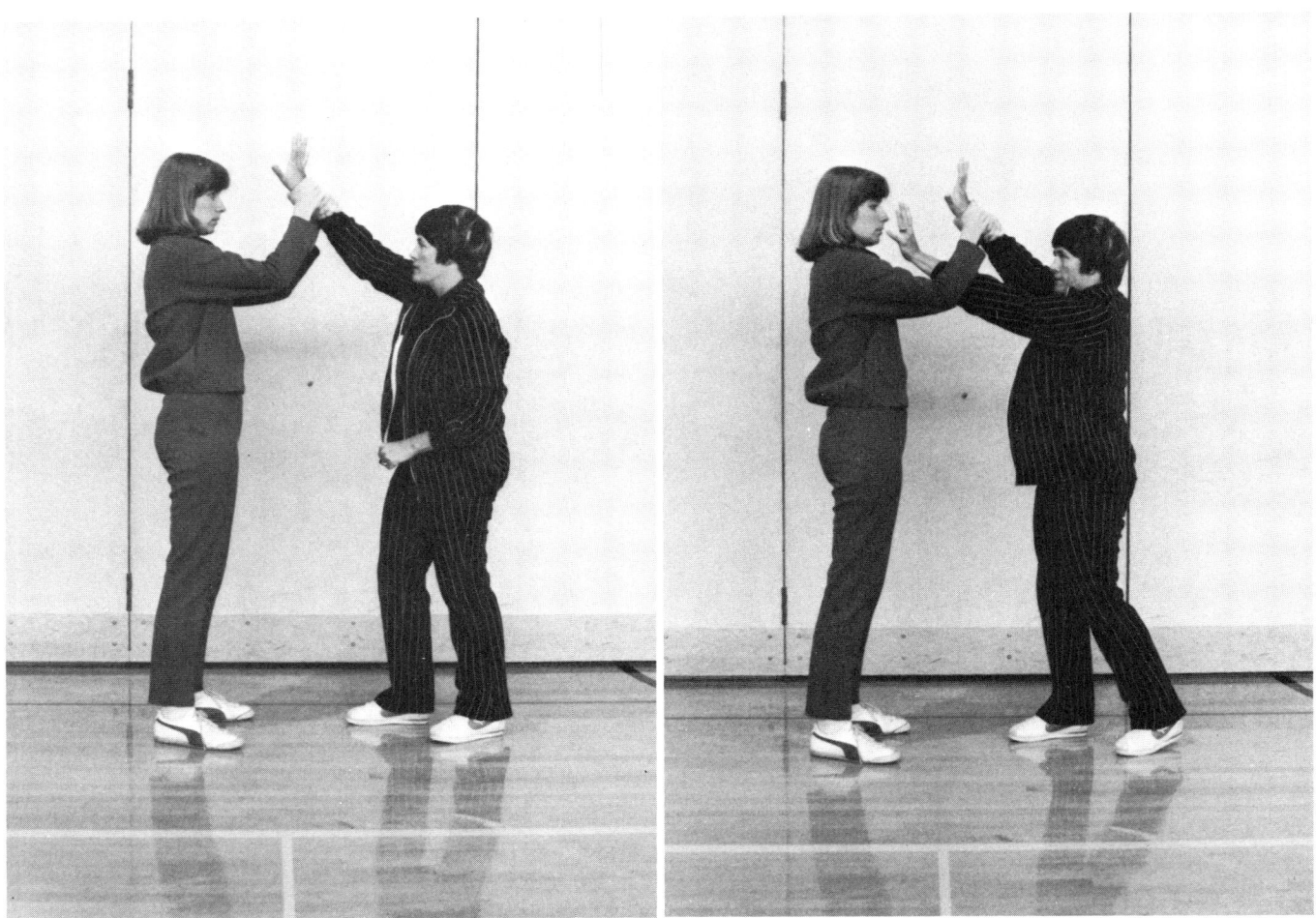

Fig. 26   Fig. 27

ESCAPE #3: TWO HANDS ON ONE WRIST, UPPER POSITION

Your wrist is being held at shoulder height or higher, figure 26.

1. DIVERSION: Loosen up the assailant by bringing your free hand up between his arms into his face or by a thrust to the groin, figure 27.
2. Reach up between his arms and grasp your gripped fist, and pull down and out against his thumbs, figure 28.
3. Step out to the side as in Escape #2, figures 29 and 30.

Fig. 28

Fig. 29

Common Faults:

- *Not taking a firm grip on your held hand.*
- *Forgetting the swing step to the side.*
- *Not pulling downward after gripping your held hand.*

Once again, practice this technique with both hands!

Fig. 30

Escape Techniques

Fig. 31 Fig. 32

ESCAPE #4: HAIR GRIP FROM REAR

1. Place your hands tightly on his, with your thumbs under his wrist, and press your head tightly against his hand, figure 31.

2. Maintaining a firm grip, roll inward towards his body (if he is holding your hair with his left hand, you will roll to the right, and vice versa, figures 32 and 33).

3. Maintain pressure against his hand with your head, immobilizing his hand and causing pain to his wrist with your thumbs.

4. He will tend to raise up on his toes to alleviate the pressure and pain and release his grip, figure 34.

Escape Techniques

Fig. 33   Fig. 34

5. In figure 34, the victim now has control of the attacker's movements. If this grip is followed through by standing completely straight, the attacker's wrist will be broken. In practice, you must stop here, when your partner is on her toes, or your partner will undoubtedly signal you to stop.

Common Faults:

- *Failure to keep a tight grip on the assailant's hand.*
- *Failure to press head tightly against his hand.*
- *Failure to maintain pressure while rolling to the inside.*
- *Forgetting to apply pressure in an upward direction.*

Remember to review with your partner your signal for release!

Escape Techniques

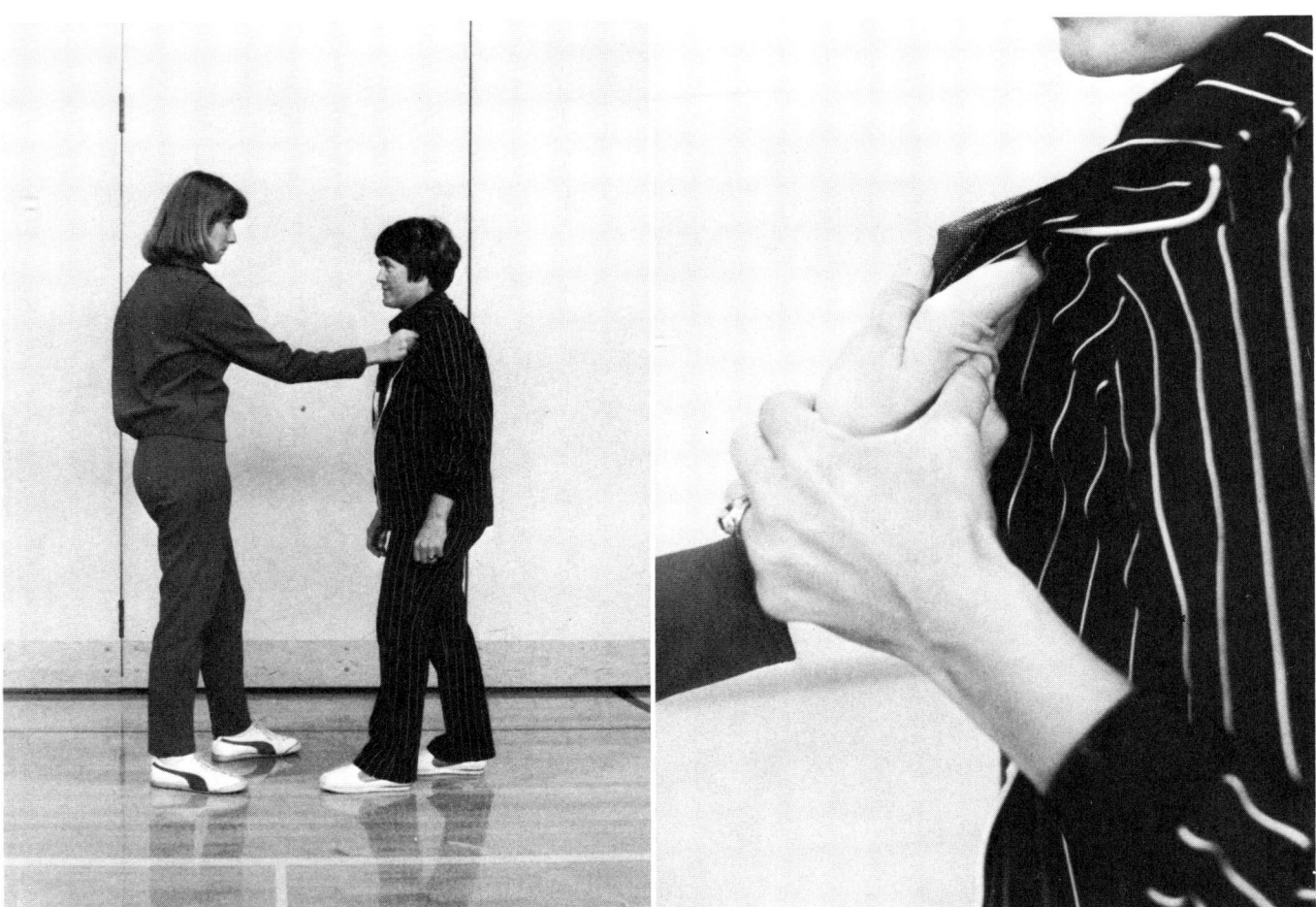

Fig. 35 Fig. 36

ESCAPE #5: THE WRIST LOCK

The assailant has grabbed your blouse, figure 35. Your method of release is:

1. With both of your hands coming toward the top side of his wrist, place your thumbs at the back of his hand, figure 36.

2. Your little fingers should be in line with the joint of his wrist and arm.

3. Using your wrists as a lever, apply pressure with your thumbs to bend his hand backward and twist it in an upward direction, figure 37.

4. His fingers will be pointing upward and, as pressure becomes greater, they will point towards his body.

A Structured Course in Practical Self-Defense for Women

DAILY LESSON PLANS

BASIC COURSE:
10 daily lessons

ADVANCED COURSE:
Lessons 11 through 27

These daily lesson plans are the result of my own teaching experiences. The need for their inclusion was made clear during the course of a national lecture and demonstration tour of colleges, women's organizations, and high schools. The first ten lessons will be useful to anyone who wishes to set up a class for women, and they can be taught without the use of special facilities. Mats are required for the remaining sixteen lessons.

If you are unsure of teaching the advanced techniques, do not go on. Seek further training if it is available in your area. I am available for workshops and may be contacted through the publisher.

In my own classes, the first session is spent mostly in discussion. I try to make everyone as comfortable as possible, and then discuss the basic definition of self-defense, the need for it, and what it means to us as women. Simple methods of protection and safety are brought to their attention by discussing everyday things, such as a set of car keys that can be carried in the hands to help ward off an attacker. It is important to make clear that assault and rape are common occurrences and can best be met if we are prepared, both mentally and physically. Mental preparedness is as much part of self-defense as the physical techniques.

Classes can vary in size from ten to one hundred, and as long as there are enough mats and space to demonstrate and practice the advanced techniques, a large class is no disadvantage in teaching or learning self-defense.

By the second session students will be ready to pair off with a partner of approximately equal size and start practicing the techniques. Practice is essential in order to create an automatic reaction in a crisis. Warm-up exercises should always be done before practicing, to loosen up the muscles. Loose-fitting clothes or sweat suits are most comfortable and easiest to work in, and tennis shoes or bare feet are preferable. When the course is complete, emphasize the need for continued practice of the techniques at home in order to maintain the speed, surprise, and efficiency needed to discourage an attacker and allow escape. There are no self-defense techniques that do not need to be practiced.

OVERALL VIEW OF UNIT Class size: 20-40 students
Time per lesson: 45 minutes

LEARNING OBJECTIVES

1. To become aware of the need for knowledge of self-defense techniques.
2. To develop mental preparedness that would cause a defensive reaction in a vulnerable situation.
3. To change any lifestyle habits that might allow one to be put in a vulnerable situation.
4. To develop body control needed to implement self-defense techniques.
5. To become proficient in self-defense techniques.
6. To learn to use speed and agility in the use of self-defense techniques.
7. To be able to make the proper reaction to a vulnerable situation automatically.

SAFETY PRECAUTIONS Many specific safety precautions are given throughout the book as they relate to specific skills. The following general rules, however, should be observed strictly throughout the unit to avoid injury or accidents.

1. Begin each class with warm-up exercises.
2. Maintain class control.
3. Methods of signaling between students during practice must be clearly understood and defined before practice begins.
4. Dress must be appropriate (i.e., tennis shoes, no belts or jewelry, and so forth).
5. Mats are needed for lessons 11 through 27.
6. Room size should allow ample space for practice without risking student safety during movement.
7. Prohibit the use of gum and candy.
8. Observe proper skill progression. Do not go on to new skills and techniques until the entire class is ready.

DAY 1

REFERENCE Chapter I, Mental Preparedness; Chapter II, What Is Self-Defense? Have students read and discuss chapters I and II or prepare a lecture on the chapters that is followed by class discussion. Go over the warm-up exercises on page 16.

NOTE Do not underestimate the need for a thorough presentation and discussion of these chapters. Many students will have stories to tell about situations they have been in. Class participation encourages their awareness. Only if the student realizes the potential number of vulnerable situations and the need for defensive measures to protect rights, body, mind, and life, will she begin to consider using the skills you will be presenting.

DAY 2

REFERENCE Chapter III, Prevention and Preparedness
Go over the points made in the chapter. Discuss with the students what habits they have that may cause a vulnerable situation and what they can do to prevent its occurrence. Ask the students to name practical items to use for self-defense that are usually carried by or available to them. If this discussion is not planned for the entire class period, it may be supplemented by the 20-minute film *Lady Beware*.

DAY 3

REFERENCE Chapter IV, Pressure Points and Vulnerable Areas

1. Demonstrate the pressure points and vulnerable areas. (5 minutes)

2. Have students warm up. (exercises, page 16; 5 minutes)

3. Pair off students.

4. Discuss a signal for stopping to be used by students when practicing. (3 minutes)

5. Begin techniques with the eyes and work downward.
    a. Discuss the eyes, making the points that they are always exposed, they water easily, and that glasses can be reached under or pulled off. Some people can't see without them. (5 minutes)
    b. Demonstrate the cupped-hand position. Do **not** have the students practice with a partner. (page 22; 5 minutes)
    c. Demonstrate nose techniques (pages 24-25; 10 minutes)

6. Have students practice eye and nose techniques. (10-12 minutes)

DAY 4

REFERENCE Chapter IV, Pressure Points and Vulnerable Areas

1. Review eye techniques, the cupped-hand position, and nose techniques in front of the class. (5 minutes)

2. Warm-ups (5 minutes)

3. Have students discuss new techniques and/or practice them in pairs.
   a. Adam's apple (page 26, 3 minutes)
   b. Collar bone: discuss part of hand to use. (page 26, 3 minutes)
   c. Elbow to the solar plexis (page 27, 5 minutes)

4. Exercise in footwork: have the students practice first in line and then with partner.
   Situation: victim grabbed around upper arms from rear.
   a. Bring elbows up to shoulder level to loosen grip.
   b. Elbow blow to solar plexis. Do more than once if needed. Victim can use both elbows alternately.
   c. Flex knees and lean forward on left or right foot. If blow with elbow is delivered with right elbow, left foot goes forward, and vice versa.
   d. With weight on balls of feet, pivot 180 degrees.
   e. Transfer weight to forward foot.
   f. With rear leg deliver blow with knee to groin area.

5. Have students practice new techniques. Do the footwork exercise to a count of four as follows:
   a. Elbows out to sides at shoulders (count 1)
   b. Foot forward, elbow to solar plexis (count 2)
   c. Pivot (count 3)
   d. Knee to groin (count 4)
   (10 minutes)

DAY 5

REFERENCE Chapter V, Escape Techniques

1. Review techniques of days 3 and 4 by practice, written quiz, or practical test-quiz. (20 minutes)
2. Warm-ups. (5 minutes)
3. Demonstrate escape #1 first without partner, then with partner. Stress safety factors and signaling methods. (pages 30-33)
4. With students standing in a circle, their feet shoulder-width apart, have them practice the escape:
   a. Thrust toward center of circle.
   b. Start turning hands so palms point toward ceiling.
   c. Snap hands outward, thumbs leading, keeping elbows close to sides.
   d. Kick backwards, taking large step to rear.
   e. Finish with both hands up, ready to strike if necessary.
5. Have students practice with partners. Correct common faults during practice. (page 32, 20 minutes)

DAY 6

REFERENCE Chapter V, Escape Techniques

1. Warm-ups (5 minutes)
2. Demonstrate escape #2. Point out that escapes 1 and 2 are possible only when going against attacker's weakest part of hand—the thumb. (pages 34-35)
3. Have students practice with partners. Correct common faults during practice. (page 35, 15 minutes)
4. Demonstrate escape #3. (pages 36-37)
5. Have students practice with partners. Correct common faults during practice. (page 37, 15 minutes)
6. Have students practice escapes 1, 2, and 3 in situations, without knowing which hold the partner will try. (10 minutes)

DAY 7

REFERENCE Chapter V, Escape Techniques

1. Warm-ups (5 minutes)

2. Demonstrate escape #4. (pages 38-39)
3. Have students practice with partners. Correct common faults during practice. (15 minutes)
4. Review in whatever manner seems most useful:
   a. Vulnerable areas
   b. Techniques in chapter 4
   c. Escapes 1, 2, 3, and 4
   (25 minutes)

DAY 8

This lesson will be a combination of review and practical application.

1. Warm-ups (5 minutes)
2. Have students form a line or circle and review the footwork exercise, day 4. Use a count of four. Then have them practice with partners, and have the victim practice going to each side with elbow and forward foot. (10 minutes)
3. One-on-one practice. Have partners practice the following situations and defense:
   a. Attack from front
   b. Attack from rear
   c. Attack while walking
   Students should consider all options of defense and yet respond quickly to gain the element of surprise. (30 minutes)

DAY 9

REFERENCE Chapter V, Escape Techniques

1. Warm-ups (5 minutes)
2. Demonstrate escape #5. Remind students to be careful, since it doesn't require much pressure to cause discomfort. (pages 40-41)
3. Have students practice with partners. Correct common faults during practice. (15 minutes)
4. One-on-one practice of all techniques. The instructor should be alert to specific situations in which students are having difficulty and direct practice when necessary.

DAY 10

REFERENCE Chapter V, Escape Techniques

EQUIPMENT Mats and masking tape. Mats hanging from the wall are best. Mark them with masking-tape Xs as targets at heights of 1, 2, and 3 feet from the floor. If wall mats are unavailable, suspend mats in some other way, such as with a vertical mat cart. Otherwise, mark the wall with masking-tape Xs and tell the students not to make contact with the wall when they kick.

1. Warm-ups (5 minutes)
2. Demonstrate snap-kick. (page 42)
3. Have students practice on their own:
    a. Assign three people per mat or one person every four feet.
    b. Have students stand one foot from mat and snap kick into mat. If mats are unavailable, have them stand far enough away so that they don't contact the wall during practice.
    c. Have students begin by aiming their kicks at the lowest target and work their way up. Highest target area represents the groin.

    (15-20 minutes)
4. Use remaining time for review, practice, testing, or the film **Lady Beware** if not shown earlier.

DAY 11

REFERENCE Chapter VI, Falling Techniques

EQUIPMENT Mats

1. Warm-ups (5 minutes)
2. Lecture on falling techniques. Stress relaxation in falling and that arms can absorb 70 percent of the fall. Students should be cautioned to keep chins tucked and shoulders rounded. (page 43, 5 minutes)
3. Demonstrate side breakfall, sitting position, to right side only. (page 50)
4. Sitting position practice: assign two students per mat, sitting at opposite ends, backs facing. Stress whiplike action of arm. The arm should finish up by the face, where it was in the starting position. Correct common faults during practice. (page 51; 10 minutes)

5. Demonstrate side breakfall, squat position, right side only. (pages 52-53)
6. Have students use the same practice position as in step 4 and correct common faults. (10 minutes)
7. Demonstrate side breakfall, standing position, right side only. (pages 54-56)
8. Have students use the same practice position as in step 4 and correct common faults. (page 56; 10 minutes)

DAY 12

REFERENCE Chapter VI, Falling Techniques
EQUIPMENT Mats

After warm-ups, follow the demonstration and practice plan for day 11, but every breakfall is to be done to the *left*.

DAY 13

REFERENCE Chapter VI, Falling Techniques; Chapter VII, A Throwing Technique
EQUIPMENT Mats

1. Warm-ups (5 minutes)
2. Review **right** side breakfalls. Students should practice at least ten falls from the sitting, squatting, and standing positions.*
3. Review **left** side breakfalls. Students should practice at least ten falls from the sitting, squatting, and standing positions.*
*Time will depend on how many mats and students you have.
4. Introduce material on throwing. (page 57)

DAY 14

REFERENCE Chapter VII, A Throwing Technique
EQUIPMENT Mats

1. Warm-ups (5 minutes)
2. Demonstrate O Goshi, face to face position. (pages 57-59)
3. Discuss center of gravity—where it is and how to use it. Discuss mechanical principles of the throw. (page 57)

4. Have students practice with partners, using the right foot step-in only. Instructor should talk students through step-ins the first ten times using the following sequence:
    a. Left hand
    b. Right hand
    c. Right arm around waist
    d. Pivot
    e. Right hip out, flex knees
    f. Step out

    Correct common faults during practice. (page 60)

NOTE Students should practice the step-in at least twenty-five times before lifting partners.

5. Have students practice the step-in and lift with partners. Instructor should talk students through the step-in and lift the first ten times using the following sequence:
    a. Left hand
    b. Right hand
    c. Right arm around waist
    d. Pivot
    e. Right hip out, flex knees
    f. Lift
    g. Set down
    h. Step out

    Correct common faults during practice. (page 60)

NOTE Students must not throw their partners until each student is capable of falling correctly and the step-in has been practiced at least 100 times. See lesson plan for day 17.

DAY 15

REFERENCE Chapter VII, A Throwing Technique

EQUIPMENT Mats

After warm-ups, follow the demonstration and practice plan for day 14 with *left* foot step-ins. (30 minutes) Have student practice with partners, switching from right to left step-ins at random. (10 minutes)

DAY 16

REFERENCE Chapter VII, A Throwing Technique

EQUIPMENT Mats

1. Warm-ups (5 minutes)
2. Have each student do ten right breakfalls each in the sitting, squatting, and standing positions; and then the same number of left breakfalls in the same positions.
3. Have students form groups of ten to twelve and stand in two lines facing each other as shown:

   Attackers: 1   2   3   4   5   6
   Victims: 7   8   9   10   11   12

   Each victim does four step-ins and lifts to the right and four to the left on the attacker facing her. Then all rotate clockwise one position. Attacker 5 then becomes attacker 6, and attacker 6 becomes victim 12 and so forth. Continue rotation until all students have returned to their starting positions. They may then switch members with another group. (30-35 minutes)

DAY 17

REFERENCE Chapter VII, A Throwing Technique

EQUIPMENT Mats

1. Warm-ups (5 minutes)
2. Determine whether or not the students are ready to take falls. If not, repeat lesson for day 16. Even if some are ready, it is best to practice for one more day.
3. If students are properly prepared, the instructor should throw the students the first couple of times. Thus the landing and body position can be checked as well as arm action.
4. After checking the students as described in step 3, have one pair of proficient students at a time demonstrate the throw. Ask the class to comment on each fall and throw. (page 60, 40 minutes)

DAY 18

REFERENCE Chapter VII, A Throwing Technique

EQUIPMENT Mats

1. Warm-ups (5 minutes)

2. Have each student do five right breakfalls each in the sitting, squatting, and standing positions; and then the same number of left breakfalls in the same positions. (10 minutes)
3. Have each student do ten step-in and lifts to the right side and ten to the left side. (10 minutes)
4. Have each student do three throws from each side, change partners and repeat until time is up. (15-20 minutes)

DAY 19

REFERENCE Chapter VIII, Advanced Techniques

EQUIPMENT Mats

1. Warm-ups (5 minutes)
2. Demonstrate O Goshi, side by side position. (pages 61-62; 5 minutes)
3. Have students begin to practice without the throw, as in O Goshi face to face position. After they do steps a and b twenty-five times with the lift, they may attempt the throw.
    a. Victim is on the left. Both partners begin on right foot, side by side, and take three steps.
    b. The victim must end up half a step ahead so that she can use the attacker's momentum to carry her partner over.
    (20 minutes)
4. When students get used to the feel of the throw, have them practice from a normal walk. (5-10 minutes)
5. Have one pair at a time demonstrate for the class, and evaluate. Check: center of gravity lowered; right hip pushed out to the right; push up from heels, knees, and hips to help swing attacker over. (5-10 minutes)

DAY 20

REFERENCE Chapter VIII, Advanced Techniques

EQUIPMENT Mats

1. Warm-ups (5 minutes)
2. Have students practice the following:
    a. Ten step-ins and lifts on right and left, O Goshi face to face position (5-10 minutes)

  b. Five O Goshi face to face throws on right and five on left (5-10 minutes)

3. Review and have students practice O Goshi side by side steps and lift, victim on left. (5 minutes)
4. Have students practice five O Goshi side by side throws from a normal walk. (10 minutes)
5. In remaining class time, have students practice O Goshi side by side position with victim on **right** side. The victim goes through the following steps with her partner, starting on **left** foot:
  a. Step in and lift twenty-five times.
  b. Attempt step-in and lift from normal walk ten times.
  c. Attempt throw.

DAY 21

REFERENCE Chapter VIII, Advanced Techniques

EQUIPMENT Mats

  After warm-ups, have students complete number of exercises assigned for step 5, day 20. Then have them do ten O Goshi side by side throws, victim on right; then ten with victim on left. Ask one pair at a time to demonstrate the O Goshi side by side throw with victim on right and then left, and evaluate. If there is any time left, have students do five O Goshi face to face throws, right and left, before leaving class.

DAY 22

REFERENCE Chapter VIII, Advanced Techniques

EQUIPMENT Mats

  After warm-ups, demonstrate the O Goshi face to face position, on the move, throwing from the right hip only. (pages 63-64) Have students note that the first step is taken with the left foot; the second step is on the right foot, which stays on the floor and is the pivot foot; and pivoting is done on the ball of the foot to the left. Students may begin practice with the throw. No lifts are necessary.

DAY 23

REFERENCE Chapter VIII, Advanced Techniques

EQUIPMENT Mats

1. Warm-ups (5 minutes)
2. Review O Goshi face to face position, on the move, throwing over right hip. (5 minutes)
3. Demonstrate how to do throw over **left** hip: first step is taken with the right foot, and second with the left.
4. Have students practice throw over left hip. (20 minutes)
5. Have students do five each of the following throws:
   a. O Goshi side by side position: victim left, then victim right
   b. O Goshi face to face position, on the move: left hip, then right hip.

   (15 minutes)

DAY 24

REFERENCE Chapter VIII, Advanced Techniques

EQUIPMENT Mats

1. Warm-ups (5 minutes)
2. Demonstrate O Goshi rear attack position #1. Throw over right hip first, then left. Have students note that victim's feet hardly move from attack position throughout attack. (pages 65-67)
3. Have students do lift position five times over **right** hip; then try throw five times. (10 minutes)
4. Have students do lift position for **left** throw five times; then try throw over left hip, five times. (10 minutes)
5. Demonstrate O Goshi rear attack position #2. (pages 69-70)
6. Have students practice position #2 and correct common faults. (page 71; 20 minutes)

DAY 25

REFERENCE Chapter VIII, Advanced Techniques

EQUIPMENT Mats

1. Warm-ups (5 minutes)
2. Review O Goshi rear attack position #1. Have students do five throws on each side. (10 minutes)
3. Review O Goshi rear attack position #2. Have students do five throws. (5 minutes)
4. Have students do five of each of the following O Goshi throws with different partners:
   a. Face to face: right and left
   b. Side by side: right and left
   c. Face to face, on the move: right and left
   d. Rear attack position #1: right and left
   e. Rear attack position #2

   (25 minutes)

DAY 26

REFERENCE Chapter VIII, Advanced Techniques
EQUIPMENT Mats and rubber knives
NOTE Use only rubber knives or other flexible objects.

1. Warm-ups (5 minutes)
2. Demonstrate knife defense attack from above. (pages 72-73)
3. Have students practice defense and correct common faults. (page 73; 20 minutes)
4. Demonstrate knife defense, straight-in attack. (page 74)
5. Have students practice defense and correct common faults. (page 75; 20 minutes)

DAY 27

UNIT REVIEW Class time may be used for practical testing, a written exam, student demonstrations, picking situations from a hat and executing the defense, and so forth. The instructor may wish to increase the number of class days to allow more practice for practical testing.

NOTES

Escape Techniques

Fig. 37

5. Elongate his biceps again by stepping backward while applying pressure.

The assailant will be easily brought to the ground with this technique, which shows that although women are sometimes as strong as men, their flexibility is often greater. With a simple leverage technique and pressure application the pain will be great on the assailant's inflexible wrist.

Common Faults:

- *Not applying pressure continually to back of the hand.*
- *Not twisting the hand and wrist to the outside.*
- *Not stepping back to elongate the muscle.*
- *Not using the little fingers along the wrist joint as part of the lever.*

Escape Techniques

Fig. 38

THE SNAP KICK

Our legs are both longer and stronger than our arms; therefore, it is to our advantage to use them in an attack if at all possible. The added length enables us to deliver a blow without putting ourselves in a vulnerable position.

The stance for the snap kick should be comfortable, with the feet shoulder-width apart. Raise the kicking leg with knee bent and snap the foot out as quickly as possible and then return the foot to the floor. Your toes should be curled and you should use the ball of your foot to deliver the blow. Kicking with the toes, especially if you are barefoot, will cause you more pain than it will the assailant.

Key words for practicing should be "up easy, kick fast, down easy." Practice with both legs. Figure 38 shows the position of the kicking leg raised right before the kick. Notice that the toes are pointing upward to enable the thrust of the kick to be delivered with the ball of the foot.

Common Faults:

- *Trying to rush the kick before we have the mechanics practiced well enough.*
- *Not snapping the foot out.*
- *Not getting the knee high enough before the kick.*
- *Not curling the toes and using the ball of the foot.*

Chapter VI Falling Techniques

Falling techniques are not only a necessary part of self-defense; they are also useful in any situation as a preventive measure against injury. Whether you are thrown in practice, are pushed down by an attacker, or fall accidentally, knowing how to fall correctly can spare you much pain and injury.

In your practice sessions, throwing your partner and letting yourself be thrown will give both of you the feel of the technique. Knowing how to break your fall and falling correctly will prevent you and your partner from injuring one another. If you are pushed down (as are many older people by hit-and-run purse snatchers), the falling techniques can save you from broken bones. Also, if you are able to fall correctly in an attack situation, you will be better able to recover and defend yourself. You may avoid having the breath knocked out of you, or injuries that would end any further defensive measures.

Finally, knowing the right way to fall can keep you from hurting yourself in accidental falls. One woman found that the side breakfall really worked when she fell off her platform shoes. In the winter, most people are vulnerable to slipping on ice or snow, or falling while skating.

The more relaxed you are, the less apt you are to injure yourself. In practicing falling techniques your objectives are to (1) be as relaxed as possible, (2) keep your chin tucked, and (3) use your arms instead of your body to absorb most of the shock.

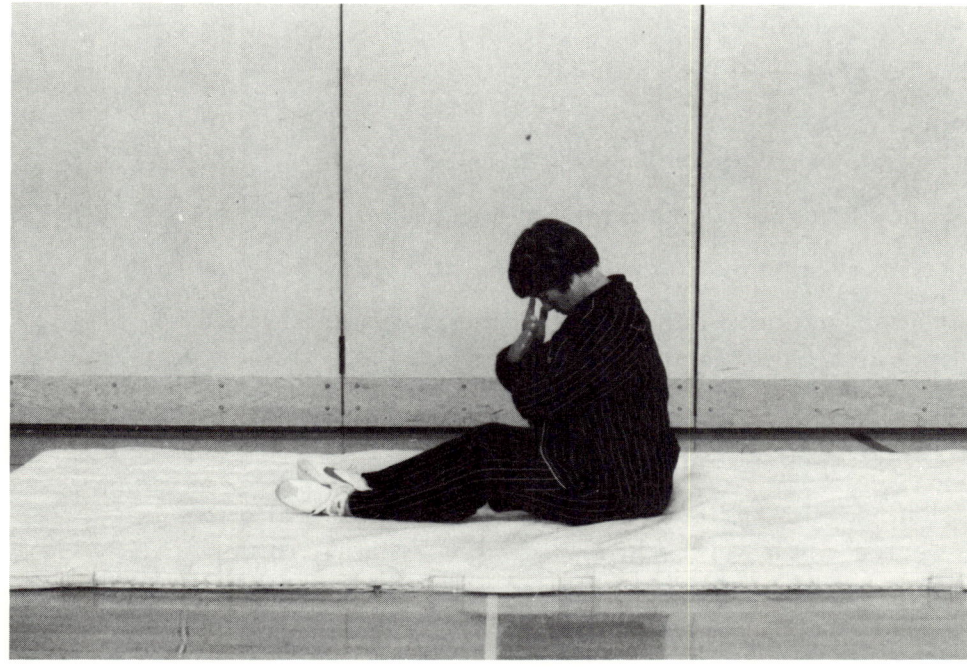

Fig. 39

Falling Techniques

Fig. 40

PHASE I: BACK BREAKFALL—SITTING POSITION

Starting Position:
1. Tuck your chin down toward the chest, figure 39.

2. Keep your shoulders rounded and remain in a tucked-in position.

3. Hold your arms straight out in front with the palms down.

4. Bring your hands toward your face, crossing your arms in front until your palms are next to your face, figure 40.

The Fall:
1. Roll backwards until your belt or waist touches the mat.

2. Both arms should simultaneously uncross and hit the mat at a forty-five-degree angle to the body, using a whiplike action, while the body continues to roll backward, figure 41.

3. Return your arms quickly to the crossed position after the slap.

Falling Techniques

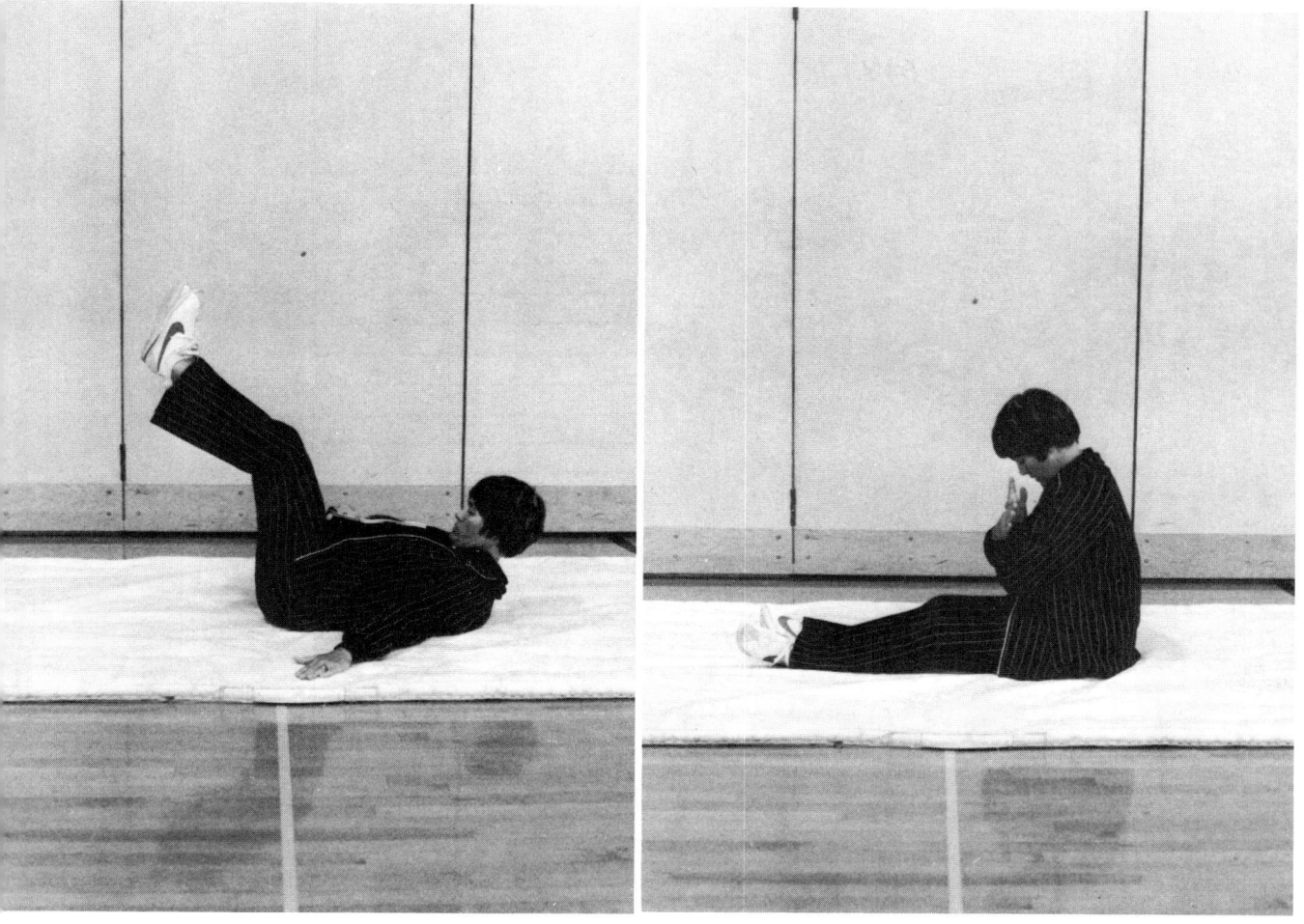

Fig. 41   Fig. 42

4. Your head must not touch the mat when rolling back—if it does, you have rolled too far.

5. Return to a sitting position, figure 42.

Common Faults:

- *Not tucking the chin tightly enough, and so causing the head to snap back.*
- *Not staying in a tucked position throughout the breakfall.*
- *Throwing the body back forcefully instead of gently rolling backwards.*
- *Not snapping the arms down and up fast enough for them to absorb 70 percent of the fall.*
- *Catching yourself with the arms instead of snapping them down.*
- *Having an incorrect angle degree between the arms and body at time of snap.*

Falling Techniques

Fig. 43

PHASE II: BACK BREAKFALL—SQUATTING POSITION

Starting position:

1. Squatting in a tucked position, fold your arms as in phase I, figure 43.

The Fall:

1. Sit down gently, with your chin and body remaining tucked, figure 44.
2. Fall backward until your belt or waist touches the mat.
3. Uncross your arms, slap the mat in a whiplike manner while your body continues to roll backward, figure 45.
4. Return your arms to the folded position immediately after the slap, figure 46.
5. Return to the squatting position.

Common Faults:

- *Same as phase I.*

Falling Techniques

Fig. 44

Fig. 45

Falling Techniques

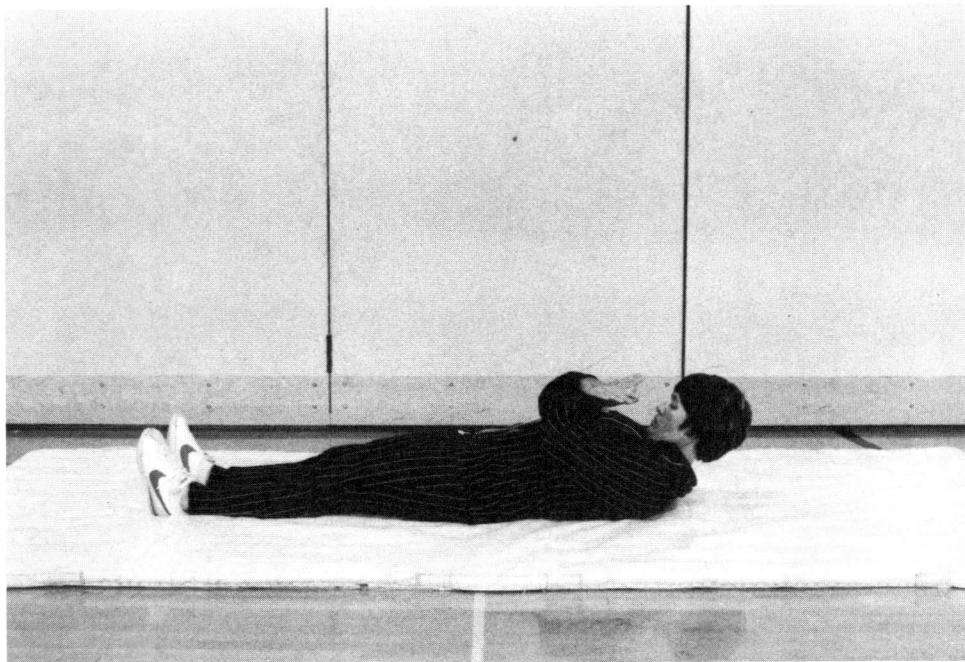

Fig. 46

PHASE III: BACK BREAKFALL—STANDING POSITION

Starting position:

1. Standing, arms crossed as in phases I and II, figure 47.

The Fall:

1. Very slowly and gently move your body from the standing position to a squatting position and finally a sitting position. This is done smoothly by keeping your hips directly underneath you and above your feet; do not bend at the waist or your loss of balance will cause you to fall quickly and land hard on the mat. Figure 48 shows going to a squat position correctly.

2. Procedure of phase II is followed once squatting position is reached.

Common Faults:

- *Same as phases I and II.*

Falling Techniques

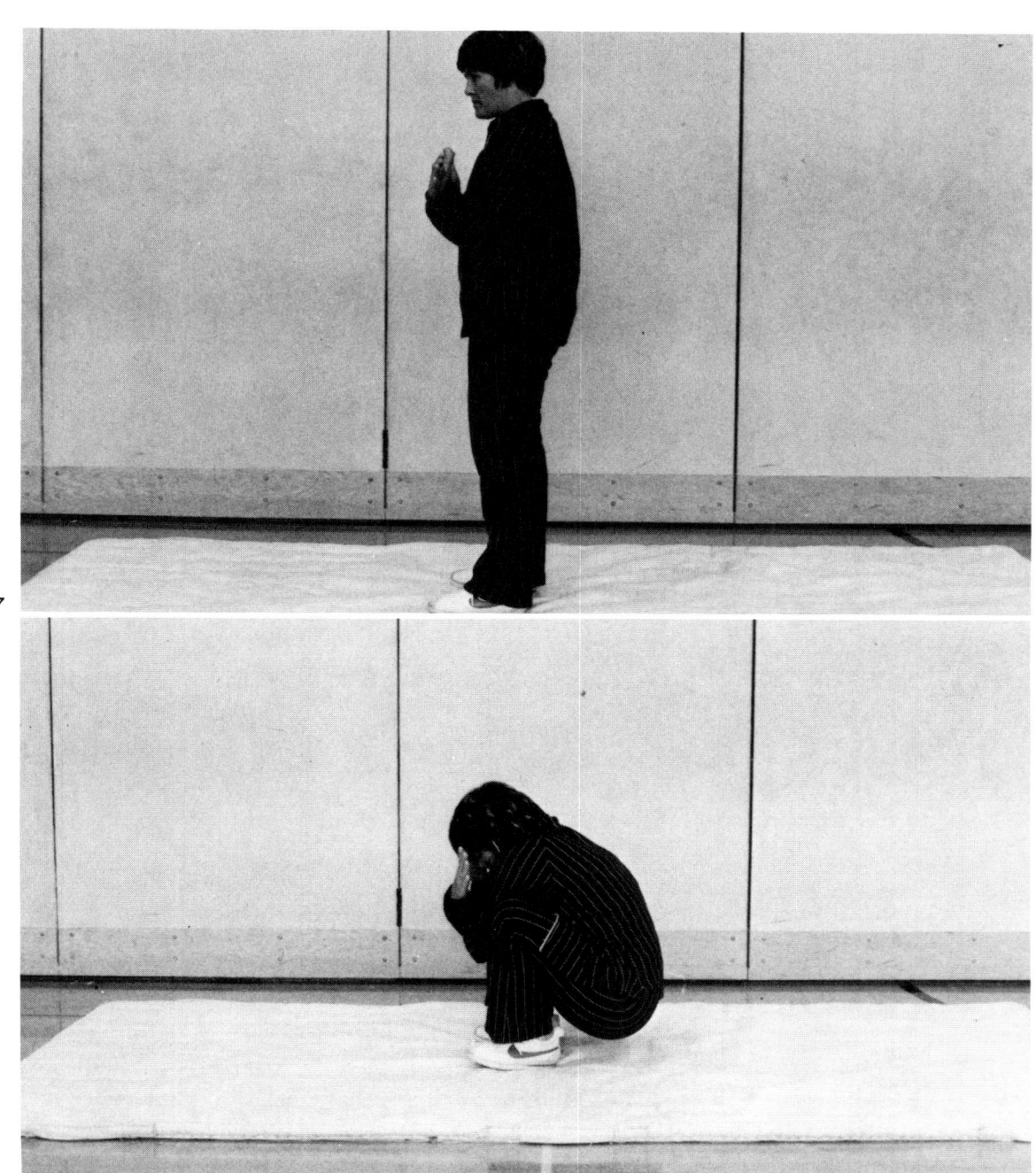

Fig. 47

Fig. 48

Falling Techniques

Fig. 49

PHASE IV: SIDE BREAKFALL—SITTING POSITION, FALLING TO THE RIGHT SIDE

Starting Position:

1. Sitting, with your chin tucked, shoulders rounded, and your left arm across your stomach.

2. Hold your right arm extended in front of you with the palm down.

3. Bring your right palm toward the left side of your face, figure 49.

4. Sit on the right back pocket of your pants, with your feet twelve to eighteen inches apart.

The Fall:

1. Keeping your body tucked, roll backward over the pocket of your pants, figure 50.

2. As you continue to roll backward, your arm should snap down and back up again in a whiplike action as your belt or waist touches the mat.

3. Your right arm should hit the mat at a forty-five-degree angle to your body, figure 51.

4. The right leg will be on the mat and the left leg slightly bent with your weight on the ball of the foot.

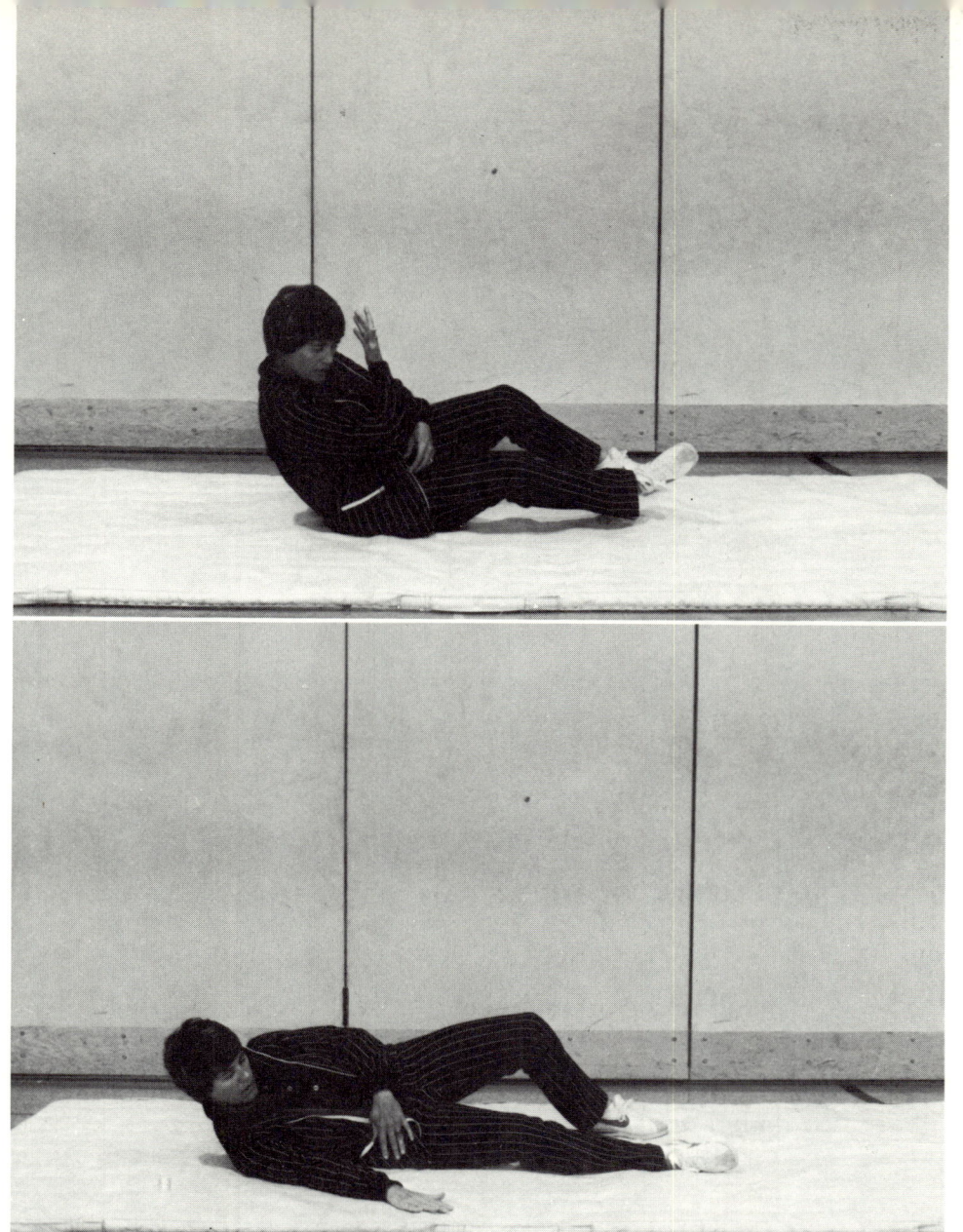

Fig. 50

Fig. 51

Common Faults:

- *Not keeping chin tucked.*
- *Not keeping body tucked.*
- *Rolling straight back, landing on your back instead of hip pocket.*
- *Hitting floor too late with arm.*
- *Uncurling body and throwing arm to mat instead of gently rolling back and slapping mat at proper time.*
- *Not keeping feet apart.*
- *Hitting knees together.*

Falling Techniques

Fig. 52

PHASE V: SIDE BREAKFALL—SITTING POSITION, FALLING TO THE LEFT SIDE

Starting Position:

1. Same as phase IV with left and right reversed.

The Fall:

1. Same as phase IV with left and right reversed.

Common Faults:

- *Same as phase IV.*

PHASE VI: SIDE BREAKFALL—SQUATTING POSITION, FALLING TO THE RIGHT SIDE

Starting Position: (see figure 52.)

1. Squat with chin tucked, shoulders rounded, left arm across stomach.

2. Using left hand for balance, put right leg straight out in front of you, resting your heel on the floor.

3. Hold right arm in front of body, palm toward left side of face (as in phase IV).

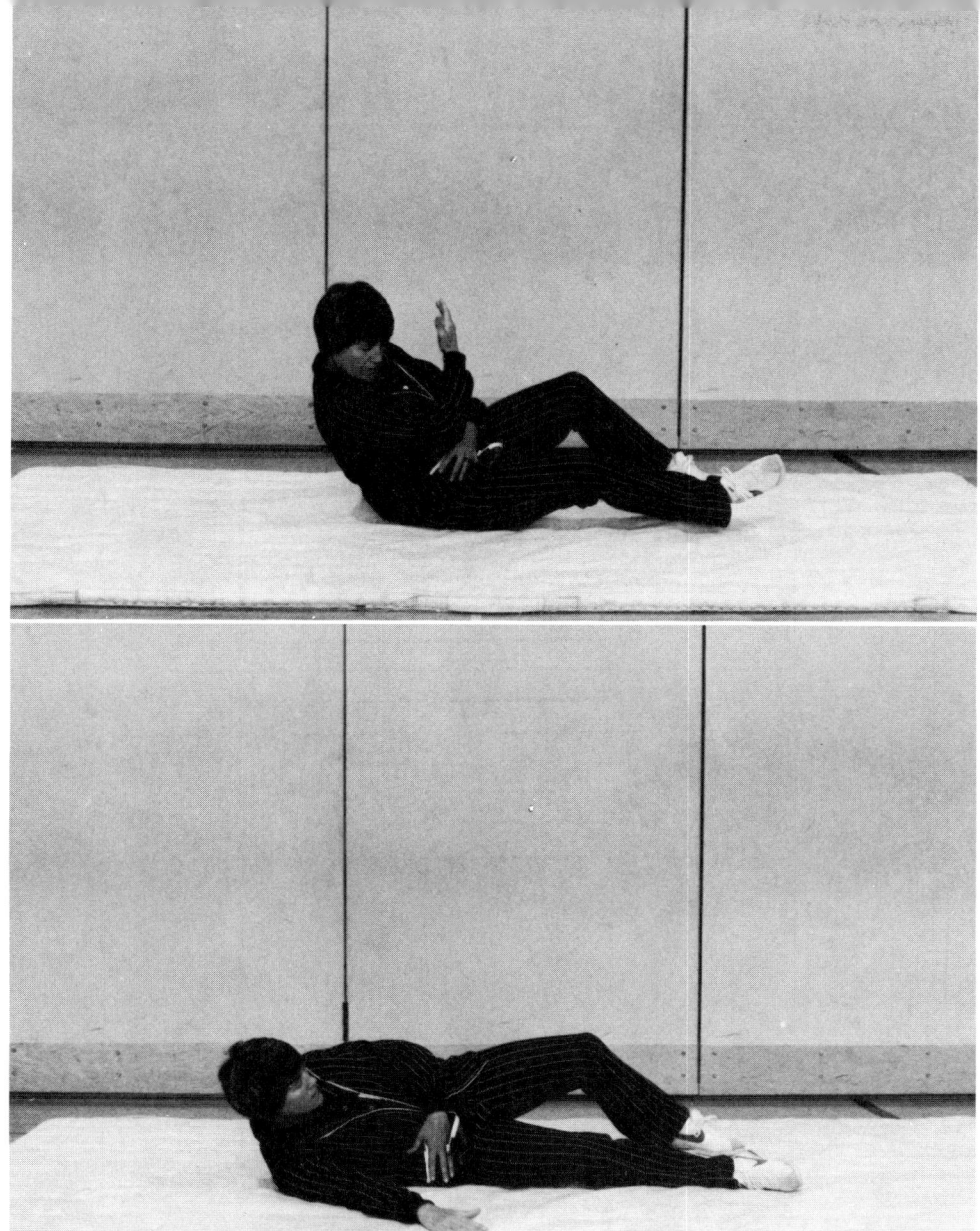

fig. 53

fig. 54

The Fall:

1. Gently sit down on your right back pocket, figure 53.

2. As you continue to roll back, snap your right arm down and up as soon as your belt or waist touches the mat.

3. Your arm should contact the mat at a forty-five-degree angle to your body.

4. Right leg lands on mat, left leg slightly bent with weight on ball of foot, figure 54.

Falling Techniques

Common Faults:

- *Same as phase IV.*

PHASE VII: SIDE BREAKFALL—SQUATTING POSITION, FALLING TO THE LEFT SIDE

Starting position:

1. Same as phase VI, with right and left reversed.

The Fall:

1. Same as phase VI, with right and left reversed.

Common Faults:

- *Same as phase IV.*

Fig. 55

PHASE VIII: SIDE BREAKFALL—STANDING POSITION, FALLING TO THE RIGHT SIDE

Starting Position:

1. Stand with your right foot forward, and right arm in position with palm toward left side of face. (See figure 55.)

Fig. 56

Fig. 57

The Fall:

1. Gently and slowly move your body from a standing position to a squatting position, figure 56, and then to a sitting position on your right back pocket.

2. Keeping your shoulders rounded and your chin tucked, roll backward until your belt or waist touches mat.

3. Snap arm down to the mat and back up again, hitting the mat at a forty-five-degree angle to your body in a whiplike action.

4. Your body should continue to roll backward until your right leg is on the mat and your left leg is slightly bent with the weight on the ball of the left foot, figure 57.

Falling Techniques

Common Faults:

- *Same as phase IV, and*
- *Not keeping your weight over your feet while going from a standing to a squatting position, causing a loss of balance and fall to the mat.*

PHASE IX: SIDE BREAKFALL—STANDING POSITION, FALLING TO THE LEFT SIDE

Starting Position:

1. Same as phase VIII, with right and left reversed.

The Fall:

1. Same as phase VIII, with right and left reversed.

Common Faults:

- *Same as phase VIII.*

Chapter VII A Throwing Technique

In practical self-defense you need a throw that is easily executed and applicable to numerous situations. It would be impractical to learn a different throw for every possible situation. The O Goshi or major hip throw, lends itself nicely to our needs because it is fairly easy to learn and can be executed from numerous positions.

Before practicing a throw the students should be proficient at the falling techniques described in chapter five. Before attempting the first throw it will be necessary to step into the position, lift your partner, and then set your partner back down on her feet, many times. Experienced demonstrators can aid the instructor as well as the students by showing the basics of the throw. Students can then be sure of the steps before the first throw is attempted.

Key points to remember before throwing someone are:
1. There are actually three parts to every throw:
    a. unbalancing
    b. moving into position
    c. the actual throw
2. It is much easier to throw someone who is:
    a. standing with his weight on his toes or his heels
    b. standing on one foot
    c. moving, since momentum helps him over

Mechanical Principles of the Throw:
1. By lowering your center of gravity below the assailant's you are able to get him off balance.
2. With the small base created by standing with the feet five inches apart, the thrower is able to set herself off balance in a forward direction when lifting. This gives the assailant forward momentum, which carries him over.
3. Hip rotation adds to the speed with which the body hits the floor.
4. By extending the hip to the side you gain rotation, force, and speed.

A Throwing Technique

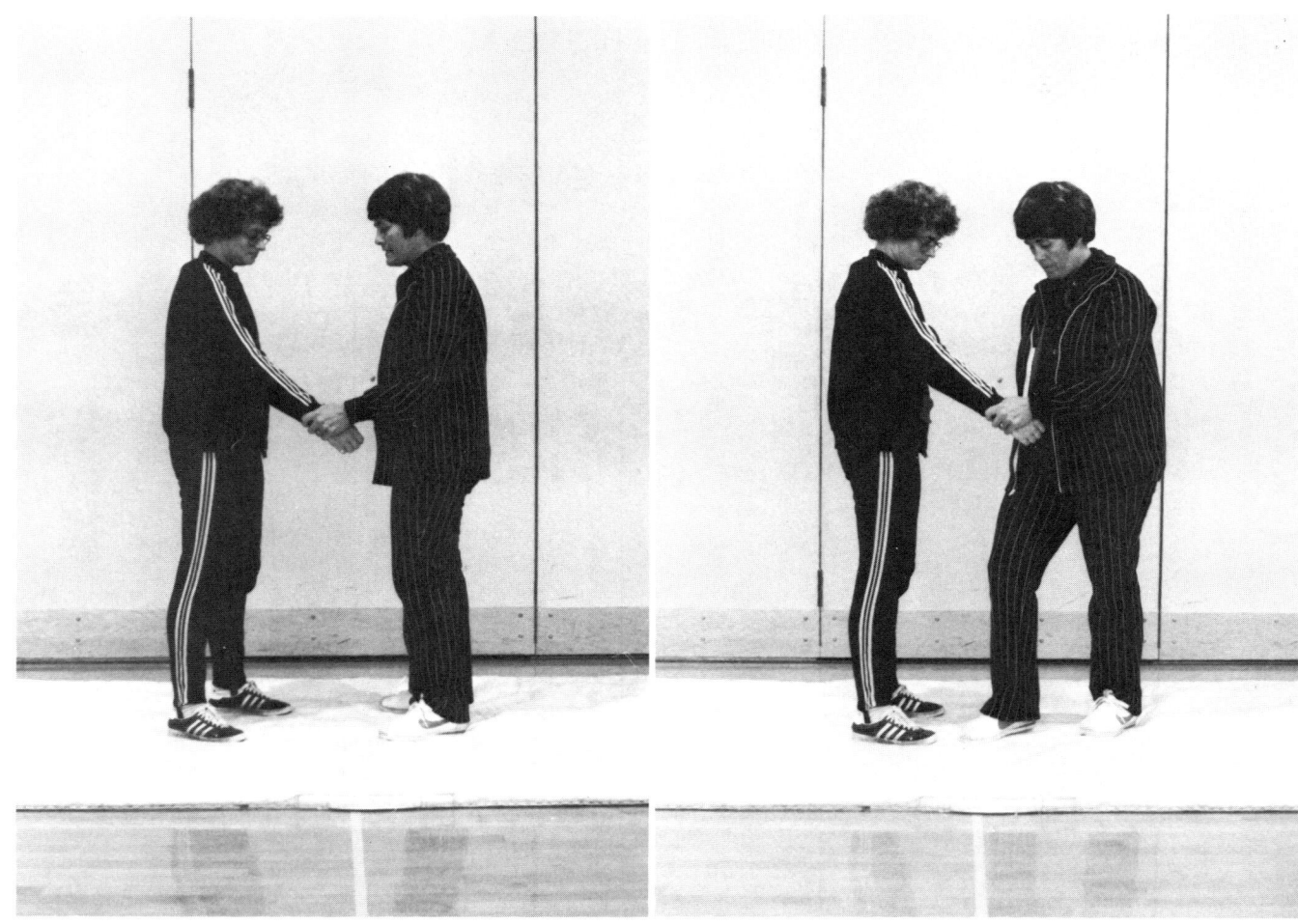

Fig. 58 Fig. 59

THE THROW: O GOSHI, FACE TO FACE POSITION

1. Stand facing each other with your feet shoulder width apart.
2. With your left hand, grip the assailant's right forearm, figure 58.
3. With your right hand reach around your opponent's waist.
4. At the same time, step diagonally across with your right foot, placing it in front of your assailant's right foot, figure 59.
5. Drop your center of gravity lower than the assailant's.
6. Pivot on the ball of your right foot and bring the left foot within five inches of the right foot, figure 60.
7. Now you are both facing the same direction and your weight is on the balls of your feet.

Fig. 60 Fig. 61

8. Extend your right hip out to the right, keeping your back straight and not bending over at the waist, figure 61.

9. Check to make sure your right arm is very tight against the assailant's waist and that there is no space between your bodies before trying to lift the assailant across your hip.

10. When lifting, the legs act like springs and straighten up, thrusting the assailant across your hip, figure 62.

11. While your hips act as a fulcrum, your left arm pulls his right arm across your stomach.

12. Look to the left as you lift and throw.

13. Your left hand never lets go of the assailant's right arm, thus giving you complete control of the assailant throughout the throw and at its finish.

14. The assailant will end up on his left side in front of you. From here you can immediately administer a kick to the groin, head, or other area to enable you to quickly let go and run, figure 63.

Fig. 62 Fig. 63

Common Faults:

- Moving the right arm from the waist position to the upper back of the assailant.
- Not having the right arm tight enough around the assailant's waist.
- Forgetting to flex knees.
- Forgetting to drop your center of gravity lower than the assailant's.
- Putting your right foot too deeply inside the assailant's feet.
- Keeping one leg in front of the other in straddle position instead of bringing both feet to within five inches of each other.
- Not having both bodies lined up and facing the same direction, which often results in pushing your hip into the assailant's stomach, thus blocking him from going over your hip.
- Not extending your hip far enough to the right side so you can use it as a fulcrum.
- Bending over at the waist instead of keeping your back straight when lifting.
- Not having the assailant's body tightly enough against your own body, causing you to strain your back when lifting.
- Forgetting to use your left arm to pull his right arm tightly across your stomach.
- Forgetting to look to the left while throwing.

Chapter VIII Advanced Techniques

Fig. 64

O GOSHI: SIDE BY SIDE POSITION

Situation:

Someone approaches you on the left or right walking in the same direction. The assailant may put an arm around your shoulder or waist.

Method:

1. Continue to walk straight ahead.

2. Slide your arm around his waist as if to encourage him.

3. Simultaneously drop your center of gravity, extend your hip into his body, and reach with your free hand across his body and grab his other wrist (see figure 64).

Advanced Techniques

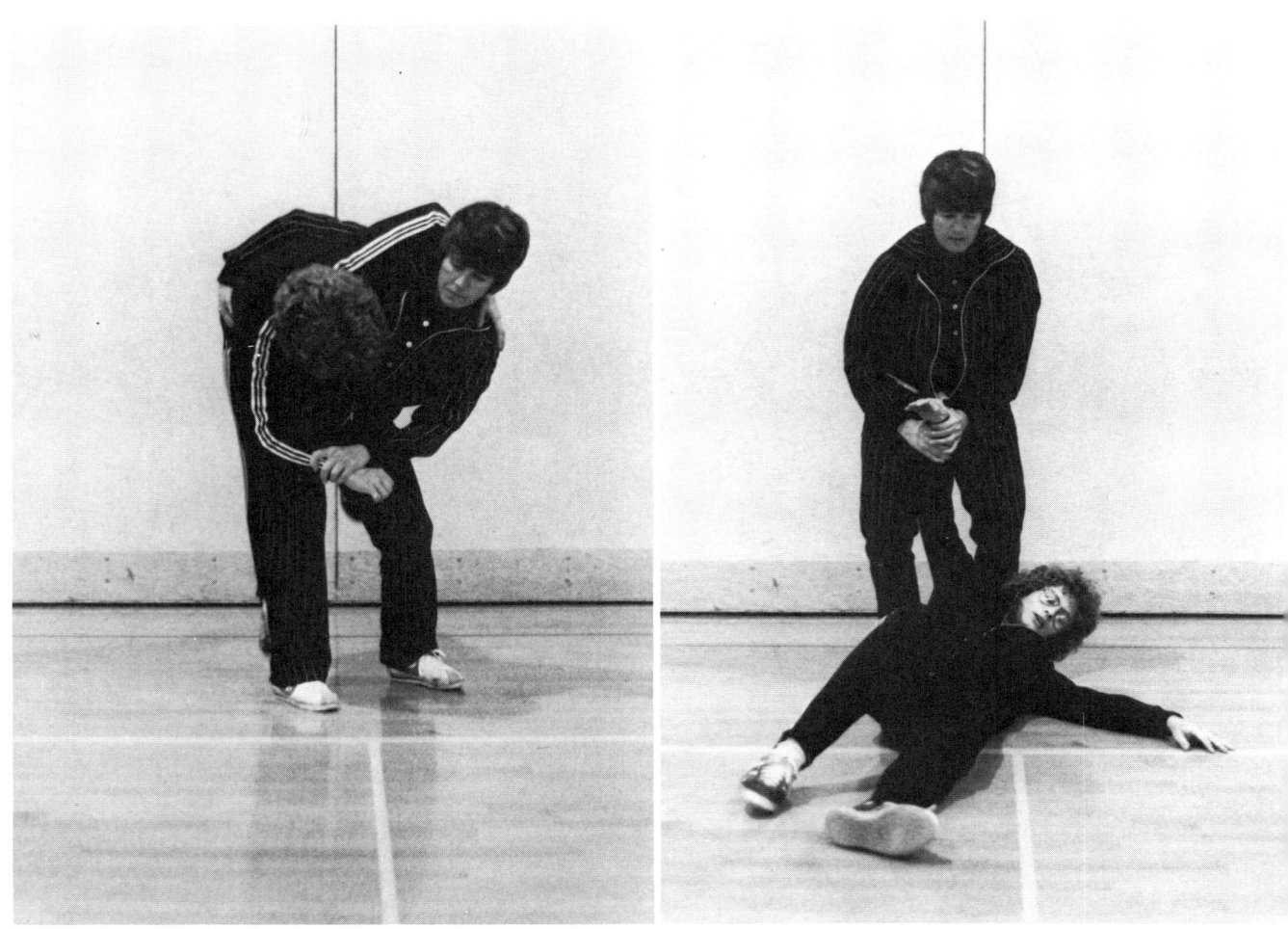

Fig. 65   Fig. 66

4. Using your hip as a fulcrum, pull the assailant over, figures 65 and 66.

Advanced Techniques

Fig. 67   Fig. 68

O GOSHI: FACE TO FACE POSITION, ON THE MOVE

Situation:

The assailant has grabbed you and is forcing you backwards.

Method of Practice:

1. Place your left hand on your partner's right wrist, figure 67.
2. While she is holding onto you, your partner should take three steps toward you, starting on the right foot.
3. You move backwards, taking your first step on your left foot.
4. Your second backward step is to your right foot, on which you pivot so you are now facing the same direction as your partner.

Advanced Techniques

Fig. 69   Fig. 70

5. Bring your left foot to within five inches of the right, as you

   a. lower your center of gravity and

   b. extend your right hip into her body, figure 68.

   c. pull your partner's right arm across your body as you bring her over your hip and to the floor, maintaining your grip on her right wrist, figures 69 and 70.

You will find that the above two throws will seem easier because they are performed on the move. A weight shift occurs as the assailant walks, making it easier to get him off balance. It is also much easier for the thrower to position herself, and the momentum carries the assailant over her hip.

Advanced Techniques

Fig. 71　　　　　　　　　　　　　　　　　　Fig. 72

O GOSHI: REAR ATTACK POSITION #1

Situation:

The assailant grabs you from behind, pinning your upper arms tightly.

Method:

1. Make him loosen his grip with an elbow to the stomach, figure 71, 72, 73.

Fig. 73

Fig. 74

Fig. 75

Fig. 76

Advanced Techniques

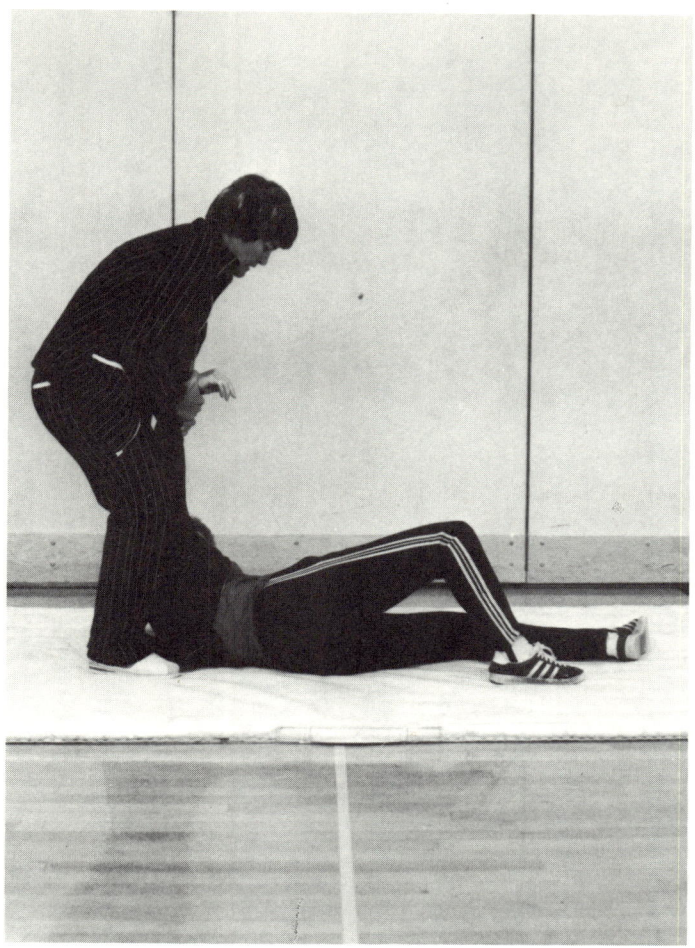

Fig. 77

2. Without changing the direction you are facing, flex your knees and slip your right arm tightly around his waist, figure 74.

3. Grab his right arm with your left hand, figure 75.

4. Extend your hip to the right and pull him across it, figure 75, 76, 77.

Advanced Techniques

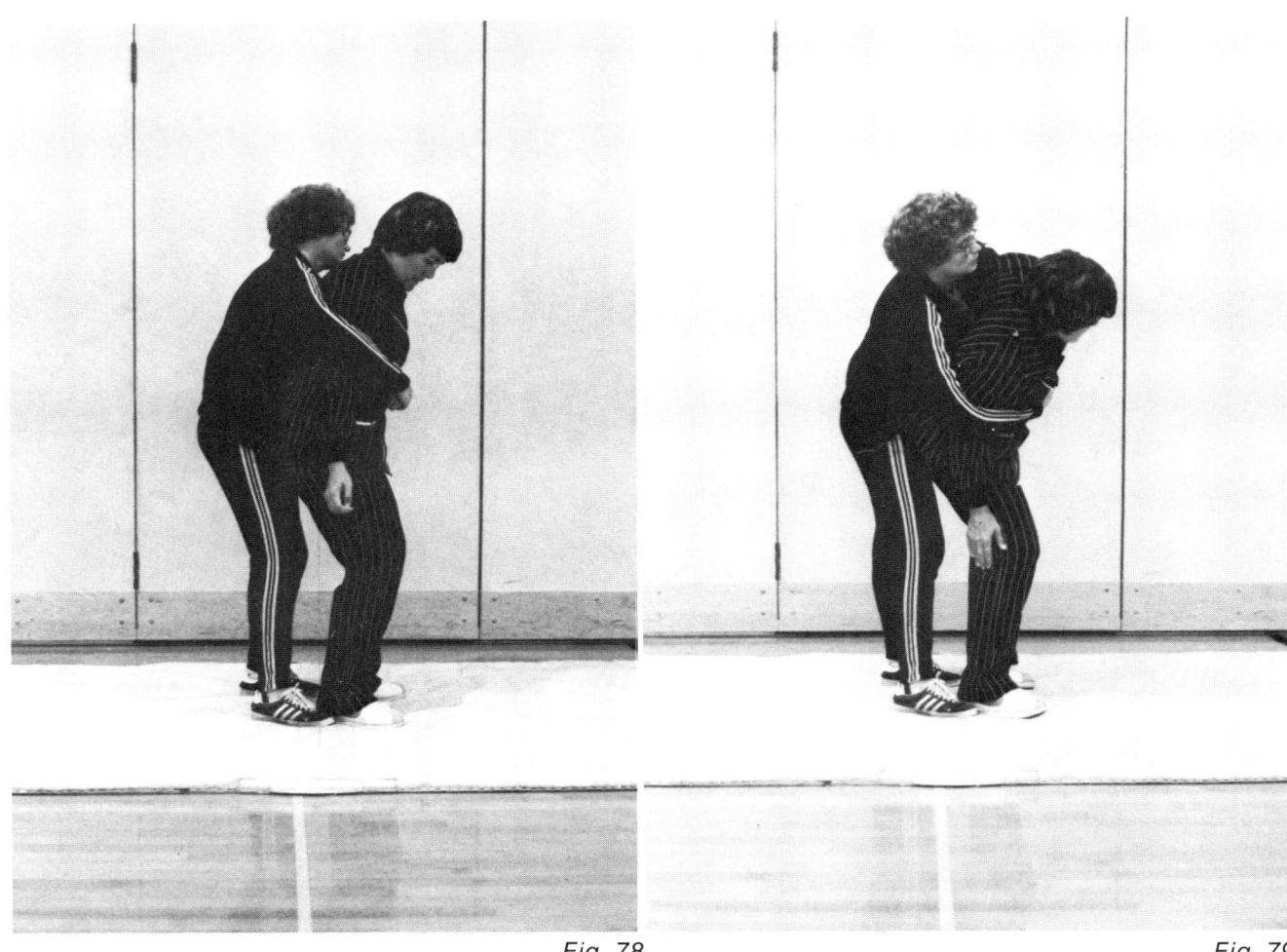

Fig. 78   Fig. 79

Note: If your arms are trapped too tightly at your side, you should:

1. Bend forward at the waist, figure 78.
2. Bend from side to side, releasing one arm and then the other, figure 79.
3. You are now in a position to use O Goshi from rear attack position #2.

Advanced Techniques

Fig. 80   Fig. 81

REAR ATTACK POSITION #2

Situation:

The assailant grabs you from behind, putting his arms around your waist.

Method:

1. Reach up and back for his face for diversion, figure 80.
2. Take a straddle step to the side, so that now one of his feet is between your two, figure 81.

Advanced Techniques

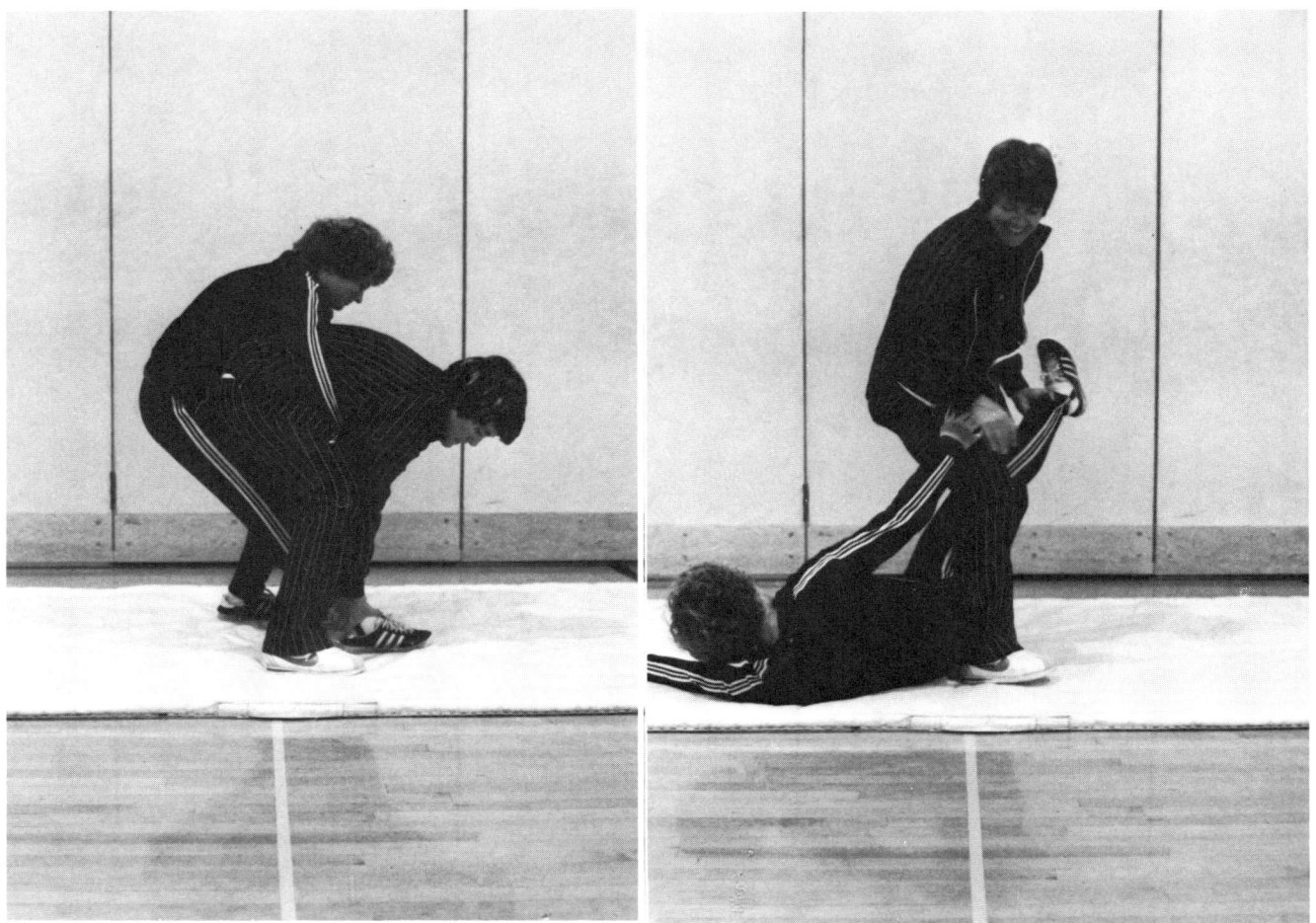

Fig. 82 Fig. 83

3. Quickly reach down and grab his heel, figure 82.
4. Slide his foot along the mat and then quickly lift it up, figure 83.
5. Continue to hold onto his foot as you turn around and plant a foot in the groin area, figure 84.

Advanced Techniques

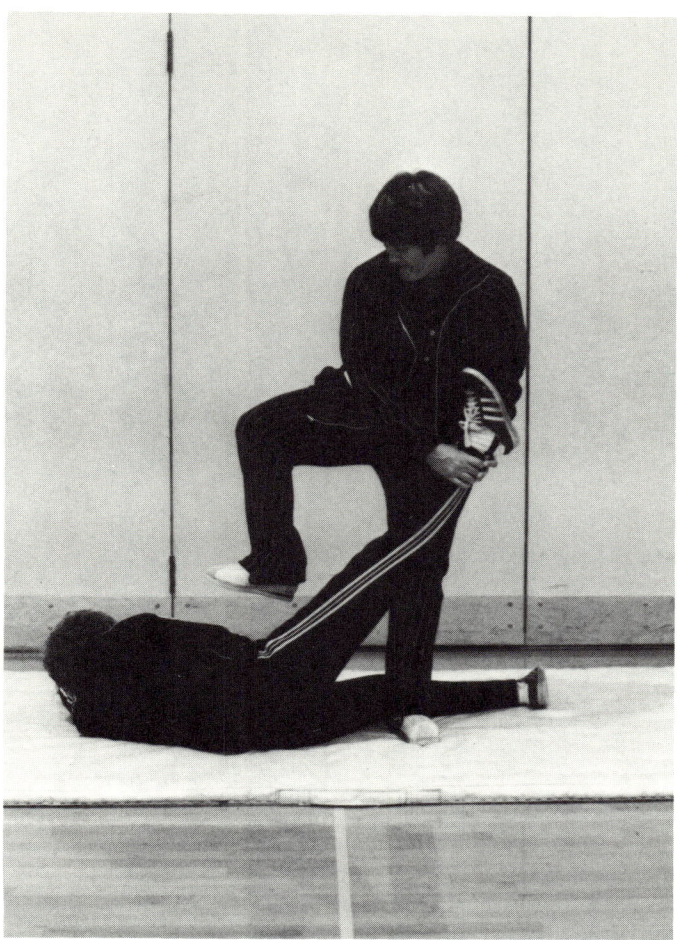

Fig. 84

Common Faults:

- Not making the reach for the eyes realistic.
- Forgetting to straddle one of his feet so that you can bend down and grab it.
- Trying to pick the foot straight up from the floor instead of first sliding it along the ground.
- Letting go of the foot.

Advanced Techniques

Fig. 85   Fig. 8

KNIFE DEFENSE

If the assailant has a knife, he will most likely attack with the knife held above his head, or by coming straight in towards your body, sometimes tossing the knife back and forth from one hand to the other.

ATTACK FROM ABOVE:

1. Step back, placing the left foot past the assailant while blocking with your left arm, figure 85. (It makes **no difference** which hand has the knife.) The block must be executed vigorously, or the force of the assailant's arm will drive the blocker's arm into her head.

2. Your blocking arm is now in front of the assailant's wrist. Slip your other arm around behind his, then grab the forearm of your blocking arm.

Advanced Techniques

Fig. 87

3. Keeping your elbows close together rather than out to the sides, bend the assailant backwards, figure 86.
4. Do **not** wait until the assailant's arm is too far down before trying to block, figure 87.

Common Faults:

- *Waiting too long to react and block.*
- *Not stepping deep enough past the assailant.*
- *Not blocking hard enough or not thrusting the blocking arm up quickly.*
- *Not grabbing your blocking arm for leverage.*
- *Not keeping your elbows down close to your body.*

Advanced Techniques

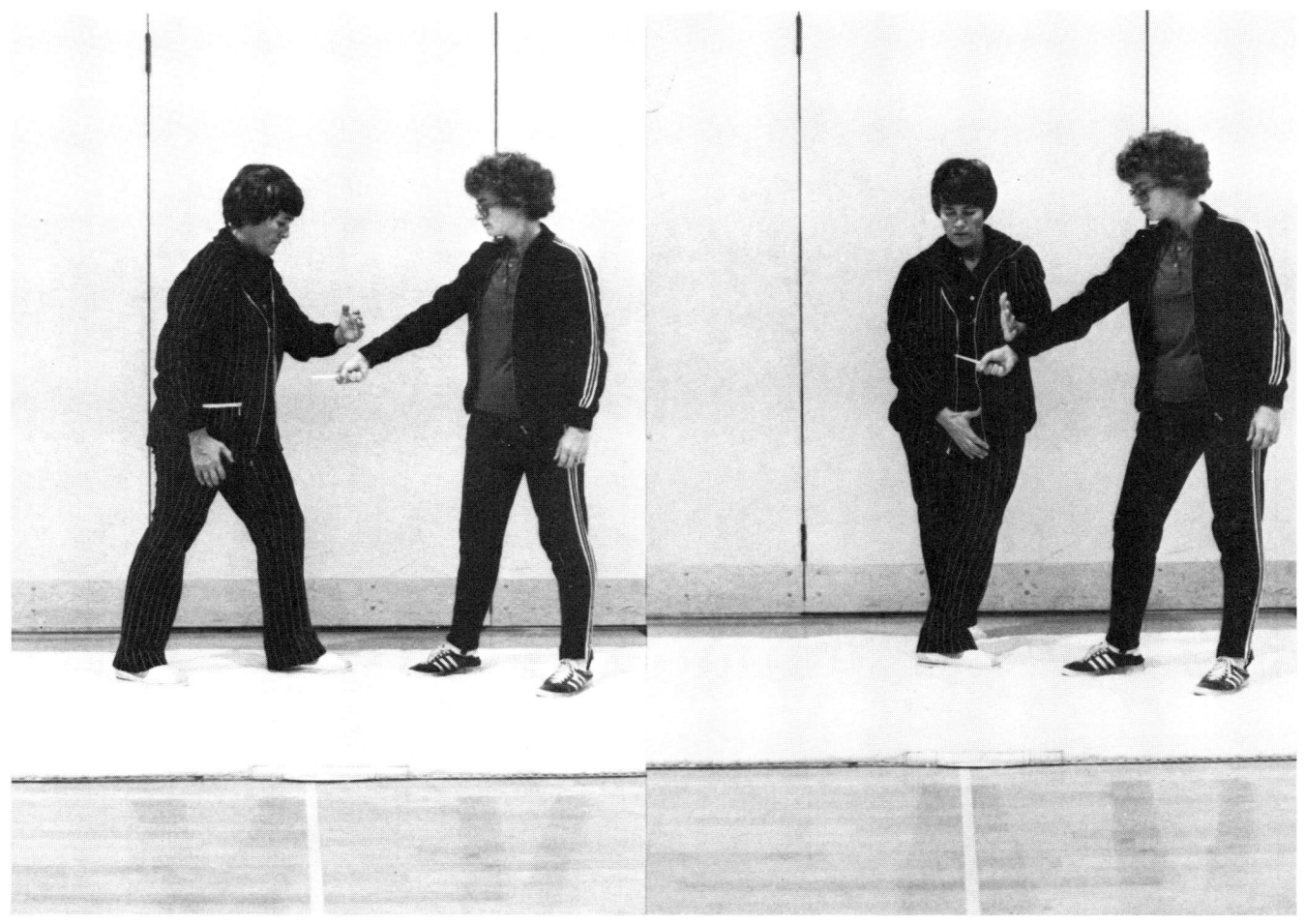

Fig. 88 Fig. 89

STRAIGHT-IN ATTACK

Method:

1. As the assailant lunges forward with the knife, figure 88, pivot on the ball of your left foot and bring the right foot back behind you, figure 89.

2. At the same time, deliver a sharp chop to the knife-hand wrist.

3. Quickly grab the back of his hand with both of yours, with thumbs on the back of his hand, figure 90.

4. Bend his hand in, so that his fingers point toward himself, and twist the wrist to the outside (figure 91), while moving backwards to elongate his arm muscles.

Advanced Techniques

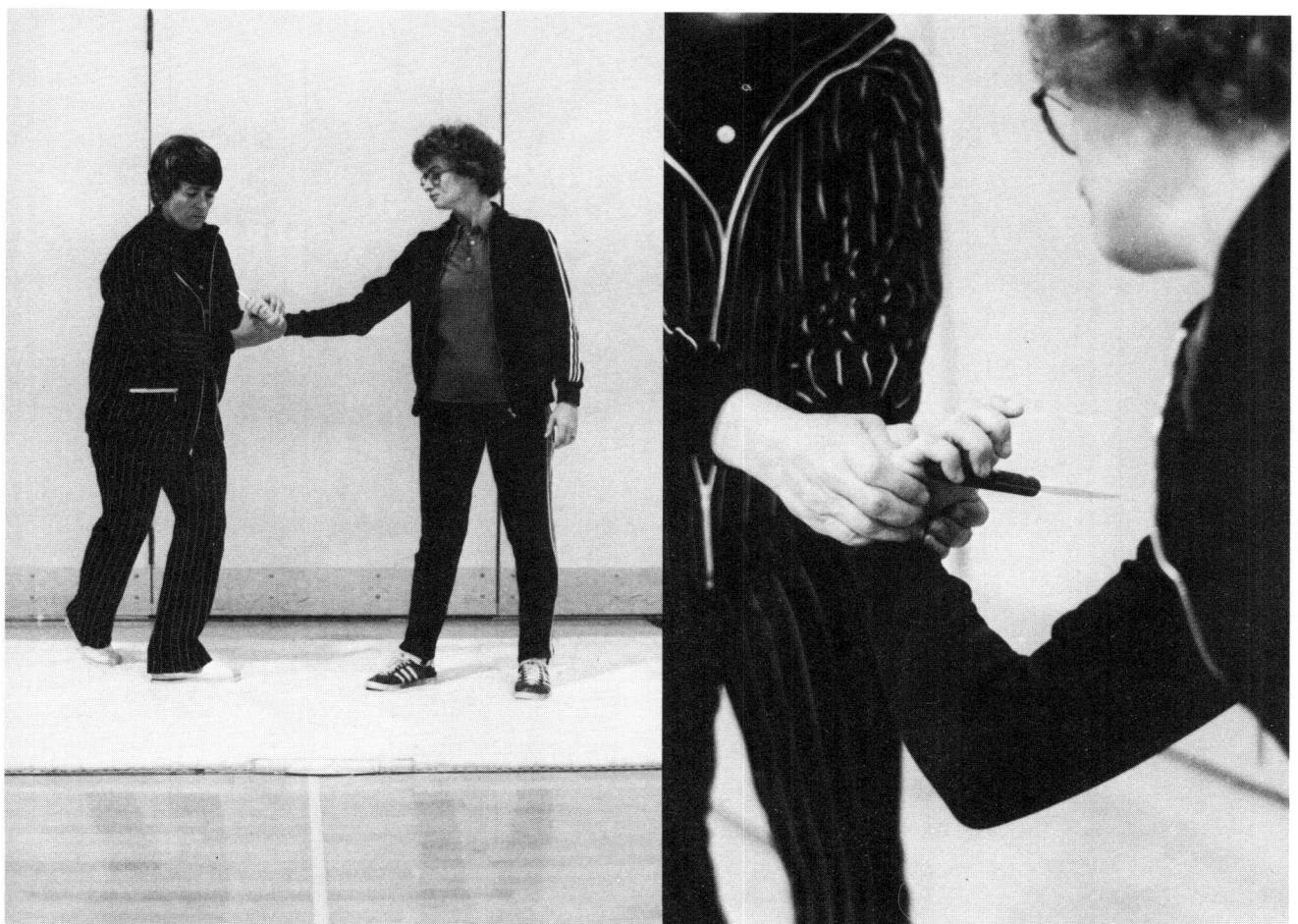

Fig. 90 Fig. 91

Common Faults:

- *Not pivoting quickly enough.*
- *Not chopping the wrist hard enough.*
- *Not going directly from the chop to the position on his hand.*
- *Not keeping pressure on the hand while twisting to the outside.*
- *Forgetting to move backwards and elongate his arm muscles.*

Chapter IX Conclusion

The first step toward practical self-defense is to be aware of the threats that exist to your safety and well-being. The newspapers are filled daily with examples of why we need to learn self-defense—purse snatching, mugging, burglary, rape, and murder. An "it can't happen to me" attitude could mean the difference between life and death, or between an actual assault and one that has been prevented by taking simple precautions. The number of violent crimes that occur in our society, and the statistics about those crimes, prove that everyone—young or old, male and female, of any race or ethnic background—is vulnerable.

However, women have some special disadvantages, particularly psychological disadvantages. Having been taught by society that they are vulnerable, women are often unable to react when their person is threatened. Overcoming those feelings of helplessness, and the paralysis that results, is one important aim of practical self-defense. Women who can react to threats of violence with a premeditated and coordinated physical response will have a significantly better chance of escaping from the situation.

The most important element of this book is, of course, prevention. Many situations can be avoided if thought is given to the circumstances. Walking home alone at night, taking shortcuts, or not locking your door when home alone, are unnecessary and avoidable risks. However, thousands of women take such risks every day. After becoming aware of the possibility of danger in these situations, the next step is to take the precautions that can prevent the danger from ever arising.

All of us should stop and consider our habits, and we will undoubtedly see some that create unnecessary risks. Some habits will have to be changed, while other situations may simply require an increased awareness of your surroundings and a general preparedness (such as carrying your keys or squeeze lemon for defense). However, preventive measures must be practiced at all times, even in your own neighborhood where you may feel safe and secure.

Another essential part of the practical self-defense program is practice. Each escape technique, fall, and throw should be practiced until you feel comfortable with it. You should be able to execute the technique without having to think about it. Your reaction must be automatic in order to be efficient. It is important to be ready at all times to meet the unexpected, and to react quickly. Being ready to surprise and outmaneuver the attacker will help make up for a difference in size or strength.

You should practice with a partner as often as possible to maintain your proficiency. Also, any kind of regular exercise is valuable in maintaining physical fitness. The more comfortable we are with our own bodies and our own capabilities, the better we will be able to react in a crisis situation. Taking only

Conclusion

ten minutes a day for exercise could greatly improve your overall physical fitness. The exercises in this manual could be used as the basis for a short and simple daily exercise routine.

The basic teachings of practical self-defense, then, combine both mental and physical preparedness. Be aware of the possibility of danger. Be alert to any potential trouble, even in areas where you feel safe. Take precautionary measures that may prevent the assault from occurring. Learn the techniques of practical self-defense, and practice them to keep your proficiency high. Expect the unexpected, even though you are taking all the precautions. Above all, be prepared to defend yourself if the unavoidable situation arises. These steps could very well save you the mental anguish and emotional stress of rape, physical harm from a would-be thief, or perhaps even save your life.

The Author

Judith A. H. Luchsinger has a Bachelor of Science degree in physical education from the University of Wisconsin. She holds the highest degree of brown belt in judo, and has taught judo and self-defense at the University of Wisconsin and through various other groups and organizations.

She has served as a consultant for the St. Paul, Minnesota Y.W.C.A. Women's Center, and as a field director on the executive staff of the Girl Scout Council of the St. Croix Valley in St. Paul. Ms. Luchsinger lives in Wyoming, Minnesota.

Practical Self-Defense for Women is available at your favorite bookstore or can be ordered directly from Dillon Press, 500 South Third Street, Minneapolis, Minnesota 55415.

TRINIDAD HIGH SCHOOL
LIBRARY